Christiane Suchanek

Digging into Chaos

Christiane Suchanek

Digging into Chaos

Security Sector Reconstruction and State-Building in Afghanistan

Tectum Verlag

Christiane Suchanek

Digging into Chaos. Security Sector Reconstruction and State-Building in Afghanistan

ISBN: 978-3-8288-4187-1
E-Book: 978-3-8288-7080-2
ePub: 978-3-8288-7081-9

Umschlagabbildung: shutterstock.com © Nate Derrick
Printed in Germany

Besuchen Sie uns im Internet
www.tectum-verlag.de

Bibliografische Informationen der Deutschen Nationalbibliothek
Die Deutsche Nationalbibliothek verzeichnet diese Publikation in der Deutschen Nationalbibliografie; detaillierte bibliografische Angaben sind im Internet über http://dnb.d-nb.de abrufbar.

Contents

List of Tables and Figures

List of Abbreviations

ANCOP	Afghan National Civil Order Police
ANDSF	Afghan National Defence and Security Forces
ANP	Afghan National Police
APPS	Afghan Personnel Pay System
AHRIMS	Afghanistan Human Resources Management Information System
ANA	Afghanistan National Army
AREU	Afghanistan Research and Evaluation Unit
CSTC-A	Combined Security Transition Command-Afghanistan
DOD	Department of Defense (U.S.)
DOS	Department of State (U.S.)
DAC	Development Assistance Committee
DDR	Disarmament, Demobilization and Reintegration
ETT	Embedded Training Teams
EU	European Union
FDD	Focused District Development
GOOD	Gender Occupational Opportunity Programme
GAO	Government Accountability Office
ISAF	International Security Assistance Force
IS	Islamic State
IS-K	Islamic State-Khorasan
KfW	Kreditanstalt für Wiederaufbau (Reconstruction Credit Institute)
MAT	Military Assistance Team
MCTF	Major Crimes Task Force
MPRI	Military Professional Resources, Incorporated
MOD	Ministry of Defence (Afghanistan)
MOI	Ministry of Interior (Afghanistan)
NUG	National Unity Government
NTM-A	NATO Training Mission-Afghanistan

NCO	Non-commissioned Officer
NATO	North Atlantic Treaty Organization
OMC-A	Office of Military Cooperation-Afghanistan
OSC-A	Office of Security Cooperation-Afghanistan
OEF	Operation Enduring Freedom
OMLT	Operational Mentoring Liaison Team
OECD	Organisation for Economic Cooperation and Development
OSCE	Organisation for Security and Co-operation in Europe
RS	Resolute Support
SFAAT	Security Force Assistance Advisory Team
SSR	Security Sector Reform
SALW	Small Arms and Light Weapons
SIGAR	U.S. Special Inspector General for Afghanistan Reconstruction
UNAMA	United Nations Assistance Mission in Afghanistan
UNDP	United Nations Development Program
UNESCO	United Nations Educational, Scientific and Cultural Organization
USAID	United States Agency for International Development
USA	United States of America

1. Introduction: Situation under Control?

The Taliban started out the year 2017 with a new offensive "Operation Mansouri" launching "the most devastating attacks on Afghan forces" (Mackenzie 2017) since the international intervention in 2001. The group announced to direct their offensive "on foreign forces, their military and intelligence infrastructure" (ibid.). The declared targets have been repeatedly under fire: In March 2017, a group of extremists disguised as doctors attacked the main military hospital in Kabul killing almost 50 people including medical staff and patients. Another grave attack was launched on April 21, 2017 when a group of at least 10 Taliban fighters attacked the Afghan army base in Masar-i-Sharif during the Friday Prayer. Disguised as soldiers, the invaders killed more than 140 Afghan soldiers (Webermann 2017).[1] Since the termination of the International Security Assistance Force (ISAF) by the end of 2014, the resurged Taliban has managed to expand its activities throughout Afghanistan (International Crisis Group 2017a, 5). At the same time, other militant groups such as the Islamic State-Khorasan (IS-K), an affiliate organisation of the Islamic State in Iraq and Syria (IS), as well as Al-Qaeda contribute to the deterioration of the situation (Otłowski 2014, 4-5).

Government officials try to calm the people. During the battles of May 2017, they explained to the residents of Kunduz "they had the situation under control" (Harooni 2017). The overall assessment of the United States' Special Inspector General for Afghanistan Reconstruction (SIGAR) indicates something different: In fact, by May 2017, the government controlled only 23.8 percent of the Afghan districts (SIGAR 2017, 88).[2] After more than a decade of international engagement and state-building efforts in Afghanistan,

1 The number of casualties varies depending on the source of information.

2 In addition, 35.9 percent of the districts were under government influence indicating a lack of authority in these districts while the central government is perceived as the dominating force (SIGAR 2017, 88).

the situation is far from being stabilized. Following the 9/11 attacks in 2001, the United States of America (USA) and the international coalition managed to overthrow the Taliban regime in Afghanistan within the first two months of the Operation Enduring Freedom (OEF). Shortly thereafter, the Afghan Interim Administration under Hamid Karzai was installed as a result of the Bonn Conference in 2001 (Hammes 2015, 278). Since then, international civilian and military assistance forces seek to advise, to assist and to reconstruct the administration system, hence the Afghan state itself. The ISAF operation and the United Nations Assistance Mission in Afghanistan (UNAMA), founded in 2002, are only two elements of the manifold international state-building and reconstruction efforts in the country (Stütz 2008, 251-253). When ISAF was terminated in 2014, signalling an end to all combat activities of the North Atlantic Treaty Organization (NATO) in Afghanistan, this was oftentimes associated with an "end of war" (Otłowski 2014, 2). Quite the opposite seems to be true given the rising number of civilian casualties recorded by UNAMA since 2009.[3] Last year, the numbers reached their current all-time high with 3,498 deaths and 7,920 injured (UNAMA 2017, 3-4).[4] The latest violent attacks, the resurgence of the Taliban, as well as rising numbers of internally displaced people and refugees indicate a deterioration of the security situation in the country – which was already the case before the completion of ISAF (Ruttig 2015). In the light of these developments, the general effectiveness and conception of international activities in Afghanistan, and, in a broader sense, state-building practices in international politics, are called into question.

The completion of ISAF was accompanied by a remarkable decline in international commitment in the country starting with the official handover of security responsibility to the Afghan government and subsequent withdrawal of substantial international troops (ibid.). Nevertheless, international forces did not leave completely due to the worsening situation. Yet the NATO's follow-up mission Resolute Support (RS) and the separate U.S.-led antiterrorism-campaign "Freedom's Sentinel" are of much smaller size (ibid.). Still, the RS mission indicates a similar strategic thrust as the former ISAF in training and mentoring Afghan security forces (Otłowski 2014, 4). The focus on the empowerment of Afghan National Security and Defence Forces (ANDSF), including the army, national police, police, and village police programme, evolved as a central pillar of international state-building pursued under the heading of security sector reform (SSR) (Hammes 2015,

3 In 2009, UNAMA began documenting civilian casualties in Afghanistan making it difficult to compare and assess earlier figures and trends (UNAMA 2017, 3).

4 This reflects the latest data available as of October 2017.

277). In view of the ongoing violent conflict, the issue of (re-)building security in Afghanistan for the state and the people remains of central importance (Hänggi 2010, 97). Despite all research conducted in this field, the lacking capacity of the Afghan state and its institutions indicate the need for further assessments of national and international efforts to foster security and stability in the country. Therefore, this study aims to answer the question: What does security sector reconstruction contribute to state-building in Afghanistan?

Thinking beyond the regional dimension of the conflict, the concept of SSR within state-building has gained importance and recognition within the international community since the 1990s (Hänggi 2010, 77). Similar reform activities have been conducted in several countries, among them, Burundi, Liberia, and South Sudan (United Nations 2013, para. 30). Thus, investigating the contribution of security sector reform includes a global rationale, without implying to generalize Afghanistan-specific findings. As Sisk (2010, 72-73) points out, it is of central importance to understand the specific (local) context of transition efforts as there is no "one-size-fits-all"-concept to state-building (Debiel and Reinhardt 2004, 536). While the definitive actions are highly context-dependent, the overarching ideal of a participatory democratic state indicates the potential of comparable research (Debiel and Rinck, Statebuilding 2017, 411)[5]. At the same time, in the field of state-building and SSR, comparative research is lacking due to its complexity and missing applicable analytical frameworks (ibid., 412). Though this paper compiles a qualitative single case study of Afghanistan, it also aims to provide an analytical framework for SSR assessment in the context of state-building that can be applied to other settings in the future.

For a start, the impact evaluation of security reconstruction in state-building requires to define the concepts of state-building in general and, in particular, of security as a state function pursued under the banner of SSR. This requires a broad literature review that delineates conceptions of the state, state-building and SSR including their theoretical and practical foundations. As any state-building approach is based on an underlying idea(l) of the state, it is crucial to embark on fundamental theories of the state in order to assess their influence on specific practices and objectives. The development of theoretical foundations requires a revision and distinction of different but

5 This ideal continues to be highly contentious. Constantini (2015, 22) emphasises that the focus on this "Weberian" model neglects the evolution of alternative forms of governance (see chapter 2).

related discourses such as state formation, peace building and nation building. Furthermore, critique to state-building and SSR has to be revealed and taken into account for the analysis.

For the purpose of feasibility, the study of SSR activities in the country is conducted two-part, focusing on two major security state actors, the police and the military. These two research objects narrow down the scope of analysis, but again come with certain constraints that are acknowledged in the theoretical and methodological chapters. First, the military and the police need to be considered as two distinct organisations based on different tasks, goals and organisational needs. These institutional differences reconsidered while analysing international efforts to re-build them. The juxtaposition of two security agencies enables a comparison between related reconstruction agendas in the same regional, historical and temporal context, but originally led by different international stakeholders. In Afghanistan, the United States headed the military reconstruction, whereas Germany took the lead for police reform (Hammes 2015, 279). The basis of different lead nations facilitates a comparison of strategies, priorities, programming and normative frameworks, which will be incorporated in the conceptual analysis.

Based on these theoretical considerations, the methodological section discusses the chosen qualitative research approach followed by the development of the analytical framework for the case study of Afghanistan that will be conducted in a next step. For the purpose of this study, Afghanistan offers a well-researched example which has been of scientific interest even before the 9/11 attacks. The very roots of the current conflict can be traced back to the colonial era or the Soviet-Afghan War from 1979 to 1989 (Hirschmann 2016, 104, Knopf 2004). While this study is devoted to the developments of the ongoing conflict since 2001, the historical and societal circumstances are included in the conflict analysis.

The study of security sector reconstruction in Afghanistan does not come without certain limitations. First, the ongoing conflict in the country hampers the documentation and verification of events, internal developments, and politics. (Giustozzi and Isaqzadeh 2013, 2). This adds to general constraints of conflict analysis facing country specific complexities like the aforementioned historical and societal peculiarities. On the other hand, the international attention concerning Afghanistan since (at least) the late 1970s has prompted various individual researchers, think tanks, governmental and non-governmental organisations to dedicate their work to this case. The Afghanistan Evaluation Unit (AREU), for example, is supporting the monitoring, evaluation and public debate about Afghanistan by providing analysis on different governance issues based upon the UN's 1998 Strategic Framework for Afghanistan (AREU 2017). As a result, there is comparably broadly available literature about Afghanistan including strategic policy analysis and first-hand field studies (e.g. by Wieker 2012 or Giustozzi and Isaqzadeh 2013). The case study thus enables to research the impact of international SSR efforts within the framework of state-building while incorporating the most recent findings.[6] In this way, it derives a critical assessment of the international agenda and the policy implications for future engagement. The last two chapters of the thesis will be assigned to the discussion and conclusion of the findings in order to draw together the main results, difficulties and prospects of the study.

6 This study was finalised in October 2017.

2. Theoretical Framework of State Reconstruction

In order to analyse the contribution of security sector reconstruction to state-building in Afghanistan, a theoretical framework is needed which defines the basic terminology and the current status of research. The state-building discourse, and beyond that the SSR-approach, consist of a theoretical and a practical dimension which are closely interconnected and imply normative considerations. In general, the theoretical pillar is based on the theory of state. This research area questions the evolution and role of the state (Stütz 2008, 33). It is crucial to first outline the theoretical foundation of the state itself as it affects the political direction of the international state-building approach and indicates the role of security (sector reconstruction). Additionally, an understanding of state theory is necessary in order to discern and assign diverging interpretations of state-building discourses, goals and practices. On the international level, the normative and practical framework for intervention and reconstruction is set out in guidelines and handbooks developed, among others, by the Organisation for Economic Development (OECD) (e.g. OECD 2007, 2008).

Starting with the basic outline of state theory, the state-building discourse is reflected and contrasted to related, but different concepts such as state formation, peace building or nation building. Although they pose distinct presumptions about decisive procedures and intended results, a review of this literature offers cross-disciplinary insights and narrows down the scope and direction of state-building activities. Moreover, these discourses present central criticisms of the state-building approach. These remarks are taken into consideration while developing the analytical framework and studying the actual implementation in Afghanistan. This aspect reflects the practical dimension of the state-building concept that is composed of field research, monitoring and evaluation of actual projects. Beyond this, the literature provides a bridge between the theoretical (and normative) considerations and real-life implementation.

As a next step, the SSR discourse will be examined in order to provide an understanding of our specific area of interest within the broader state-building debate. Again, the literature consists of theoretical and practical dimensions. In contrast to the overarching state-building literature, the SSR-track focuses closely on the role of security, its domain, scope and implementation in reconstruction agendas (e.g. by Hänggi 2010).

The introduction of the different concepts and terminology provided in this chapter creates not only a basis for analysis, but integrates this study in the scientific debate. As described above, the study incorporates primary and secondary literature from various sources, including newspaper and scientific journal articles, multilateral handbooks, and research publications in order to provide sound analysis results and outline the current state of knowledge and discussion. The key findings of the review presented in this chapter will guide the subsequent analysis. Therefore, the last section of this chapter summarizes and outlines the main results relevant for the conceptual framework.

2.1. State Theories and Definitions

2.1.1. Central Principles of State Theory

The state as a polity is not a modern invention, but, as Fukuyama (2005, 1) puts it, dates back some 6,000 years to the first Mesopotamian societies. Hierarchical orders and trained bureaucracies have already existed for thousands of years in China or Egypt (ibid.). The political organisation described as a "state" covers a great variety of different structures and thus definitions and models (Nelson 2006, 7). In order to discuss the state-building approach in international politics, a common understanding of the state and its main characteristics is necessary.[7] This section aims to provide a basic overview of common state definitions, hence attributed key functions and related controversies that translate into state-building discourses.

Starting into understanding the "state" as a concept, the Oxford Dictionary of English provides the definition that a state is "a nation or territory considered as an organized political community under one government" (Stevenson 2010, 1741). A similar definition is presented by the World Bank's World Development Report of 1997:

7 Only a selection of characteristics and historical benchmarks is presented in this chapter as the formation of state theory and related philosophy constitutes a vast research area on its own including a great variety of state definitions and models.

> "State, in its wider sense, refers to a set of institutions that possess the means of legitimate coercion, exercised over a defined territory and its population, referred to as society. The state monopolizes rulemaking within its territory through the medium of an organized government." (World Bank 1997, 20)

Therefore, the state features some kind of organisation over a geographical entity (the territory) or people (the "nation") led by the decisions of its central institution (the government). In order to enforce its rules, the government is fitted with the monopoly on legitimate[8] use of force which indicates its superiority. Common state theories regularly comprise these elements of the modern state, though with different accentuations (Stütz 2008, 34-35).

Parallels to these characteristics of the state are found in the writings of state theorist Georg Jellinek. According to Jellinek (1914, Chapter 13), a state comprises three fundamental elements: a given territory ("Staatsgebiet"), a population ("Staatsvolk") and authority over both[9] ("Staatsgewalt"). In this view, the term "Staatsvolk" is inextricably linked to a common feeling of society, i.e. the nation (Jellinek and Jellinek 1914, 407). In contrast to this, the Oxford's basic definition states "nation or territory" (Stevenson 2010, 1741). This illustrates Conrad Schetter's (2005, 8) critical remark that the classical model of the nation state – referring to Jellinek – has been turned upside down. In today's world, state borders and nations are not congruent anymore (ibid.). Still, the necessity of congruency between state, nation and territory remains an issue of discussion and leads to confusions between state building and nation building concepts.[10] This stems from diverging interpretations of the nation-term itself. Even though there is no ultimate definition for a nation, it is in a broadly speaking sense constituted by a common identity of people which may derive from cultural, ethnical, religious or political affiliation (Stütz 2008, 43-45). These multiple sources of identity may be fraught with tension leading to violent conflicts of people within a certain territory and on the academic level, to the debate about the relation between the state and the nation.

Nevertheless, Georg Jellinek's key elements of the state provide a basic understanding of state characteristics which can be related to the history of the "modern" state system. The evolution of today's conception of statehood has been the result of a violent process which culminated in the Peace of

8 As pointed out below, the concept of legitimacy is a highly contested concept (Eabrasu 2012, 208).

9 The state exercises authority over anyone staying in its territory whether they belong to the state population or not (Jellinek and Jellinek 1914, 394).

10 See section 2.2.

Westphalia in 1648 (Hirschmann 2016, 19). That date represents from a political scientist's view the codification of the main principles of contemporary international law around the globe. The principle of state sovereignty was contracted which established the internal and external self-determination of each nation state within its territory. It implies the legal application of force in the interest of the state and the equality of each state in the international system (ibid.). This aspect is explicitly emphasised by German sociologist Max Weber:

> "Today, however, we have to say that state is a human community that (successfully) claims the *monopoly of the legitimate use of physical force* within a given territory. Note that 'territory' is one of the characteristics of the state. Specifically, at the present time, the right to use physical force is ascribed to other institutions or to individuals only to the extent to which the state permits it. The state is considered the sole source of the 'right' to use violence." (Weber 1946, 77)

Similar to Jellinek, Weber includes the elements of territory, people, and authority in his definition, while he emphasises the legitimate use of violence as an exclusive right of the state (ibid.). He accentuates legitimacy as the belief in the rightful dominance of the superordinate state power which can be derived by traditions, charisma or accepted legal rules (ibid, 78-79). In a Weberian sense, the "legal domination" of the "modern state" represents the most advanced form of legitimate authority featuring a commitment to rational, law- and knowledge-oriented administration (Sisk 2013, 47-48).

Weber's definition of the state constitutes a central reference for political sciences and sociology (Eabrasu 2012, 187-188). The Weberian model is of fundamental importance as an ideal type for institutions within the state-building agenda. When the literature discusses the Weberian state or bureaucracy, it means a certain set of features. In detail, it signifies a governmental organisation structured by a hierarchy of formally separated offices with specialised tasks. These offices operate impersonally while resting on rules and regulations. Furthermore, the Weberian state applies qualification-based selection and promotion processes of bureaucrats (OECD 2009, 38-39). However, Weber's concept of legitimate rule does not read without criticism. On the one hand, the centrality of the state's monopoly of legitimate use of force has the advantage to be applicable to the multifaceted manifestations of political organisations called states. On the other hand, this definition has an intrinsically normative notion, while the essential concept of legitimacy itself poses a contested concept (Eabrasu 2012, 207-208).

Legitimacy can be roughly divided into an external and internal notion. External legitimacy derives from the recognition of a state by other states in the international system. Internal legitimacy is based on the endemic belief of rightful governance which constitutes a quite challenging concept (Hirschmann 2016, 21, Rocha Menocal 2011, 1721). A state may enjoy international recognition, i.e. external legitimacy, without owning internal legitimacy in the sense of the approval of its citizens or even without being able to effectively govern its territory (Hirschmann 2016, 21). Sisk (2013, 50) observes, that a state constitutes "very much the product of constructed realities over the years" meaning that the international recognition of a state has never been revoked even in cases like Somalia where state-structures have been almost completely decayed. As Hirschmann (2016, 11) points out, the international assumption that there is a congruency between a certain territory and one responsible government is de facto not valid anymore – taking a similar stance as Conrad Schetter (2005, 8). The formal definition of the state (territory, population, government) does not capture the reasons for state formation and preservation in the sense of stability. Weber's contentious concept of the state highlights legitimacy as a central clause to "the right to rule based on consent of the governed" (Sisk 2013, 46). This implies that a state needs to provide certain services and characteristics in order to prevail as a political form of human organisation.

2.1.2. Core Functions of the State

Departing from the definitions of the state as outlined above, there are certain qualities which are assigned to states, i.e. features that a state must provide in order to persist. These core functions of states are determined by the question, why states evolved in the first hand. There are different theories answering this puzzle that mostly rest on the writings of Thomas Hobbes and/or John Locke. Although there are certain differences in their tenets, both philosophers emphasise a "social contract" between the society and the state which constitutes mutual rights and obligation, hence core functions of the state to legitimize itself (Hirschmann 2016, 12, 21). In Hobbes' thinking, without a state people are caught in a "war of every one against every one" (Hobbes 1894, 66). In this State of Nature there is no security for anyone as there is no superior penal power safeguarding individual rights (ibid., 66-67). In his philosophical view, men gave up their ultimate freedom in the State of Nature by founding the state in exchange for the provision of security. This is the constitutive moment of the state for Hobbes, and its most profound function as the "commonwealth" loses its legitimacy when it can no longer provide for the security of its subjects (ibid., 152).

Although John Locke's perception of the State of Nature is a more positive one, he too emphasises the assignment of natural freedoms to the state in exchange for the protection of core individual rights such as life and property (Hirschmann 2016, 21). The state needs to fulfil the expectations of its subjects by carrying out the tasks assigned to him in order to demand their obedience (Stütz 2008, 50-51). Consequently, submissiveness, hence legitimacy, and ultimately statehood are continually reproduced between the society and the state (Zürcher 2005, 13).

Based on these philosophical theories, four key functions of the state are emphasised in the literature: security governance, political governance, socio-economic governance and administrative governance (Hirschmann 2016, 22-23, Debiel and Reinhardt 2004, 526). The first refers to the effective protection of the state and its subjects, i.e. the provision of security. Political governance includes the legitimacy of political processes through participation and respect for the rule of law. Socio-economic governance involves the creation of social welfare via service provision and reallocation of resources (e.g. by taxation) for education, the economy or other social goals. The fourth key function describes the administrative capacity of the state to enforce laws and legislative decisions (ibid.). These core functions are of paramount importance for the state as their accomplishment determines the administration's legitimacy, i.e. rightful governance in the eyes of its citizens (Hirschmann 2016, 23). Conversely, deficits in these essential tasks have been identified as sources of state fragility (Rocha Menocal 2011, 1715).[11]

Aside from this, there are various theories of possible and/or vital key functions that vary in their scope and ambitions, but usually contain the aforenamed four. The World Development Report of 1997 presents an array of functions ranging from "minimal" to "intermediate" to "activist" (World Bank 1997, 26-27). Fukuyama (2005, 10-11) interprets this axis as ranking from most necessary to desirable to optional. Most notably, the four abovementioned core functions can be attributed to the "minimal", thus most fundamental functions of the state, although their interpretation might vary in scope to the most optional ("activist functions").

The study of the state as a concept and attributed key functions revealed a great range of interpretation at its very basic definition. These variations of scope and assigned tasks of the state reflect the controversies over the appropriate size and strength of the state in politics of the twentieth century and

[11] See section 2.2.1 for the state fragility debate and state-building as its countermeasure.

beyond (Fukuyama 2005, 3). In addition, they also mirror fundamental disputes over the direction and extent of state-building measures which is discussed in the next section.

2.2. The "Art" of State-Building

2.2.1. State-Building on the International Agenda

Entering into state-building as a concept on the international agenda, there are diverging views about when the approach was applied the first time. Krause and Mallory (2010, 2) argue that state-building was already undertaken in the 19th and early 20th century in cases such as Greece, Belgium, Albania, Germany and Japan. In contrast to this, Stütz (2008, 20) declares state-building as a relatively new policy in international relations. These diverging interpretations about the origins and practices of state-building derive from different definitions of the concept, as well as its demarcation to the term "state formation" as we will show next.

To start with, virtually all definitions of state-building pronounce a common objective: the creation of state institutions (Eriksen 2016, 2, Fukuyama 2005, xvii). [12] In doing so, state-building as a political concept can be rooted within the branch of institutionalism in the theories of International Relations (Costantini 2015, 29). Nevertheless, the definitions vary in the attributes assigned to the institutions to (re-)build, as well as the actors declared responsible for the endeavour. Fukuyama (2005, xvii) provides the broadest notion of state-building described as "the creation of new government institutions and the strengthening of existing ones". Yet this definition is intrinsically vague: It does neither contain certain qualities, thus controllable attributes of the institutions, nor define the actors in charge of the project. Additionally, Fukuyama's definition may be applied to state-formation processes that most authors clearly mark off or oppose to the state-building approach. The term "state-formation" is used to describe a historical process "through which states evolve, independently of any particular policy or intention" (Eriksen 2016, 2). By contrast, state-building is ascribed the political intention, i.e. the purposeful action to create institutions (ibid.). This distinction is important as scholars like Kai Hirschmann (2016) or Conrad Schetter (2005) derive their critique towards state-building efforts from the violent history of state-formation. This relates to Charles Tilly's claim that

---

[12] It needs to be noted that the term "institution" is not clearly defined and may range in its interpretation from political institutions codified by law to informal everyday practices (Fukuyama 2005, 39)

"war makes state" (Tilly 1985, 170) denying that the process can be engineered peacefully or in any way successfully from the outside. Tilly's observation of violent state-formation still holds for more recent examples such as Timor-Leste (1999), although it is per se not sufficient to account for the entire spectrum of these processes today and is clearly linked to observations of the European state-formation history in the 16th and 17th century (Debiel and Rinck 2017, 408).

Empirically, the track record of international efforts to (re-)build states are "mixed at best" (ibid., 404). The evolution of the modern statehood took centuries, hence a quick but full-featured installation of such a complex entity appears illusionary or even presumptuous in the view of certain scholars (Schetter 2005, 9-10). The timeframe of state-building procedures poses indeed a central challenge to donors, practitioners and target groups alike. Evidence has shown that transformation takes a generation as even the fastest-transforming countries have needed between 15 and 30 years to increase their institutional performance above the threshold of "good enough governance" (World Bank 2011, 10 & 108).[13] Although all parties engaged in state-building seem to be aware of this long-term horizon, the short-term nature of donor states' election periods, the costs of long-term interventions, as well as the allegation of overly paternalistic programmes creates serious headwind for durable engagement (Krause 2010, 168). Therefore, it is necessary to lower overly ambitious expectations about state-building results within a short time-span instead of rejecting the whole approach without being able to provide viable conceptual alternatives (Debiel and Rinck 2017, 410, Barton 2010, 31).

The practicability of state-building efforts remains controversial in itself. There is, however, an underlying consensus that state-building cannot be done without including and orienting towards the society. This reflects the major criticism of Eriksen (2016, 3-4) that previous institution-centred approaches ignored state-society relations and the necessity of social transformation for sustainable state-building. The critique is nothing new to the international debate on state-building and has already led to a re-evaluation of existing state-building models and practices in academic research, but also within the international organisations executing such efforts.[14] Already in

---

13 "Good enough governance" is based on the concept of Grindle (2004) which is defined as "minimally acceptable government performance and civil society engagement that does not significantly hinder economic and political development" (526).

14 The incorporation of state-society relations in state-building approaches, nevertheless, does not automatically lead to its effective (or even actual) implementation. In addition, Eriksen (2016, 12) denies that this kind of social transformation can be steered from

2009, the OECD's Development Assistance Committee (DAC) published a report on concepts and dilemmas of state-building that presents a refined definition of the approach:

> "We propose to define state building as purposeful action to develop the capacity, institutions and legitimacy of the state in relation to an effective political process for negotiating the mutual demands between state and societal groups. (...) Successful state building will almost always be the product of domestic action, but it can be significantly enabled by well-targeted and responsive international assistance." (OECD 2009, 72)[15]

Therefore, state-building does not refer to a simple 'top-down' approach focusing on the state, its institutions and elites, but emphasises in particular the interrelations between state and society associated with 'bottom-up' perspectives (Rocha Menocal 2011, 1719). The OECD's definition also reflects the controversial basic assumption that outsiders can positively assist and affect the domestic construction of a state (Sisk 2013, 8).

Reviewing the different definitions of state-building, the diverging interpretations of the approach as "relatively new" (Stütz 2008, 20) or rather classical (Krause and Mallory 2010, 2) can be assigned to a poor distinction between state-formation and state-building discourses. With this fundamental distinction, the international shift towards state-building can be traced back to the 1990s when a "renaissance" or "(re-)discovery" of the state was declared (Rocha Menocal 2011, 1718).

Predominant in the 1980s and 1990s have been liberal ideas to reduce the size and authoritative control of the state (Fukuyama 2005, 5). The kick-off for the international reorientation towards state-building was related to the recognition of increasing intra-state conflicts and state fragility after the collapse of the Soviet Union (Hirschmann 2016, 14). While there is no universal definition of state fragility, weak or fragile states are generally characterized by a lack of state authority or control over their territory, lack of internal legitimacy and the incapability of government institutions to exercise the aforementioned essential state functions (Rocha Menocal 2011, 1715). Though there are multiple reasons for state-failure, some of its underlying

outside. The OECD, on the other hand, takes the view that it is difficult, but not impossible (OECD 2009, 14). This point fundamentally affects prospects of international state-building projects and thus political willingness to participate at such, which is why it needs further attention and evaluation within our study.

15 Still, this definition remains vague and problematic, e.g. in its perception of legitimacy, the appropriate role of international actors, or the meaning of "well-targeted" assistance which continue to be controversial aspects of state-building.

root causes date back to the original construction of some states under colonial rule (Debiel and Reinhardt 2004, 528). During that time, the "Western" state model was exported by the European colonial powers to the territories subjected to them. This has led to a global distribution of the organisational model without questioning the suitability for the respective culture or region (Hirschmann 2016, 12). The creation of such "artificial states" has been accompanied by arbitrary, politically guided border demarcations separating historically grown tribal areas, for instance in the case of the Afghan-Pakistan border through Pashtun homelands. This example illustrates the imposition of colonial motives on the governed territories which structurally undermined state legitimacy from the very beginning resulting in fragile and oftentimes undemocratic regimes (ibid., 12-13, 34).

Cases of violent conflicts resulting from the disintegration of those states have already been observed during the Cold War era (Debiel and Reinhardt 2004, 528). Put simply, the bipolarity in the international system suppressed the outbreak of latent regional strife and stabilized the established fragile structures. Yet with the end of the bloc confrontation in the 1990s, its disciplinary power also vanished, the conflicts erupted and state failure moved into the spotlight of the international community (Hirschmann 2016, 13-14). In the following years, the United Nations (UN) expanded the number and intensity of their peace missions aiming beyond ceasefires to a peaceful transformation of the states in focus. These peace missions included mandates for state-building activities which was perceived as a mean for facilitating stability in conflict-affected regions (Debiel and Rinck 2017, 406).

Since then, "institutions matter" has been the dictum in the international community, expressing the conviction that institutions are the decisive key to stability and development (Fukuyama 2005, 28-29). Empirical evidence for this assumption is presented, among others, by Acemoglu and Robinson (2013, 372) whose core thesis is that nations fail today because of what they call extractive institutions. In contrast to inclusive institutions, these structures systematically favour small proportions of the society (i.e. the ruling elites), do not guarantee property rights and fail to provide incentives for economic undertakings leading to economic stagnation and ultimately state failure (ibid., 429-430).

Under the headline of "good governance" the centrality of well-managed political institutions – exceeding the economic perspective – has been established as a core slogan of international development politics. The original terminology had been introduced by the World Bank and was further refined by the OECD DAC in the early 1990s (Schmidt 2013, 284-285). In contrast to the neglect of the state in the 1980s, the "good governance"-paradigm stressed the need for effective, in a normative sense "good" state institutions which has been largely accepted (yet not undisputed) by donors and scholars alike (Debiel and Rinck 2017, 405).[16] The World Bank demonstrates this conviction in its World Development Report of 1997, declaring that "development without an effective state is impossible" (World Bank 1997, 25). This dogma shifted the focus to activities subsumed under "state-building" as a collective term for various political, social and economic programmes which are oftentimes closely interrelated (Ghani and Lockhart 2010, 12-13). This bulk of activities contains headings like "capacity building", "institution building" or "(good) governance promotion" which concern various issues such as gender equality, environmental management, or disarmament, demobilization and reintegration (DDR) of former combatants, and so on (Fukuyama 2005, 28).

Concerning the different interpretations of state-building as a classical or recent concept, as outlined above, the shift in emphasis, research and scale of activities labelled state-building since the 1990s give the impression of a "new" agenda. Since then, the demand for such activities seems rising rather than diminishing related to the recognition of increasing state fragility (Krause and Mallory 2010, 1). Although the effectiveness of purposeful state-building remains a central dispute in academic debates, there are empirical findings that ungoverned territories, as well as fragile or weak states are a breeding ground for violent conflicts, organised crime and terrorism (Hirschmann 2016, 17, 51). Such effects tend to spill over to adjacent territories and ultimately develop international destabilising fall-outs most visible in growing numbers of refugees (Collier, et al. 2003, 33). This also holds for the Afghanistan conflict whose dimensions can even be observed in Europe, where the number of Afghan refugees increased up to around 800.000 until 2015 according to UN-estimates (Ruttig 2015). International intervention is thus inherently driven be a domestic imperative calling to manage external risks.

The main roots of international security threats have shifted from inter-state wars to growing intra-state strife. This development points out that internal conflicts and state fragility are mutually dependent as they originate from the construction of government organisations themselves (Hänggi 2010, 79). This changed the probabilities and rules of peace as research has

[16] There is no consistent use of the "good governance"-term in international politics. Yet there are common elements usually attached to the concept laid out by the World Bank or the OECD DAC. These include an enhancement of public management, accountability of governance on all levels, rule of law, fighting corruption, enhancing transparency, the acceptance of human rights, and democratisation (Schmidt 2013, 285).

found that a country that had suffered from violent conflict is most likely to relapse into internal war. Paul Collier (et al. 2003) labelled this phenomenon the "conflict trap", observing that countries that had experienced a civil war have a chance of 44 percent of relapsing into conflict within a five-year period (Collier, et al. 2003, 83). This finding has been confirmed and even observed worse: 90 percent of the last decade's civil wars are a recurrence of internal strife over the last 30 years (World Bank 2011, 2). Regarding this problem, state-building serves as a strategy to break these "vicious cycles of conflict" (Sisk 2013, 4). Yet, the analysis of state-building on the international agenda has revealed controversies concerning the concept's direction and effectiveness which are contrasted to other "building"-concepts in the following section.

2.2.2. Contrasting State-Building

In this section, the state-building approach is contrasted to other related but different conceptions. The distinction of discourses serves to clarify the research focus of this study and illustrates main threads of discussion concerning the state-building approach.

To start with, state-building is neither peace-building nor nation-building. All of these "building"-approaches have in common that they comprise a broad set of activities and notions (OECD 2009, 13). However, they stress a different focus in attention that becomes apparent when defining the terms. Peace-building activities focus primarily on the sustainable institutionalisation of peace including both the "negative" notion of the absence of violence, and the "positive" notion of producing inclusive, participatory politics (Call and Cousens 2008, 3-4). Apart from this, the concept of "nation-building" refers to a set of strategies with the ultimate goal of creating a common national identity based on a cultural, ethnical, political or historic narrative (OECD 2009, 13). Nation-building might serve the programme of state-building as it aims at mobilising loyalty to the state-project based on the idea of a nation (Hirschmann 2016, 22). The focus of state-building is different as it concentrates on administrative institutions. Anyhow, related activities might take existing identities into consideration and ultimately, yet not necessarily, produce a nation state (Stütz 2008, 21)

Although the distinction of the terms reveals initial differences, there are some entanglements between them. First, while the definition of nation-building today explicitly refers to the creation of a public spirit, the expression has been used synonymously for state-building activities in the past – more concretely before the 9/11 attacks in 2001 (Berger 2006, 5-6). The designation "state-building" has been established as a substitute term for nation building as it was perceived "less problematic" and "more acceptable" due to a more technocratic than normative connotation (ibid., 5-6 & 13). As shown above, state-building is neither a simply technocratic approach in the sense of focusing solely on the functioning of state institutions without relating to the society, nor without normative assumptions of ideal states. Yet, it is important to notice that the terms have been used interchangeably in pre-9/11 documents and might still be confused today despite their different focus in attention.

Secondly, state-building is considered to have evolved as an alternative to the peace-building approach (Sisk 2010, 58). According to this narrative, the prominence of state-building has emerged from the recognition that peace-building methods omitted government-related dimensions (Rocha Menocal 2011, 1718). The history of purposeful state-building can, nevertheless, be traced back further into the past than this narrative, focusing on the shift in international politics in the 1990s, suggests.[17] In addition to the different perspectives of the concepts, highlighting them as alternatives to each other triggered the ongoing debate around their exclusiveness or compatibility (Grävingholt, Gänzle and Ziaja 2009, 1). This discussion encompasses useful remarks on the main difficulties within (post-)conflict environments. For example, it stresses that contesting power groups fight for their own maximalist victory, i.e. full political power, not for a power-sharing compromise and that the contests of election may produce new conflicts instead of peace (Sisk 2010, 64). However, both state-building and peace-building have changed, broadened and balanced their original programme, dissolving the exclusionary juxtaposition in theory and practice (Grävingholt, Gänzle and Ziaja 2009, 1). Similar to the discourse on nation-building, state-building has faced allegations of constituting a technocratic and apolitical exercise in contrast to peace-building (Sisk 2010, 71 & 74). Yet in international state-building today, there is a distinct emphasis on the role of civil society, the historic legacy of institutions, as well as social and political structures reflected by the OECD's "Principles for Good International Engagement" (OECD 2007).

Conversely, the peace-building approach has too broadened its scope by increasingly acknowledging the role of states for the establishment of sustainable peace (Grävingholt, Gänzle and Ziaja 2009, 2). The rebalance of these two "building"-discourses resulted in a practical convergence of their agendas, action-guiding principles and areas of engagement (ibid., 1-2). Despite this common ground, it is still important to be aware of the tensions and

---

17 See section 2.2.1 for the origins of state-building.

criticisms on the original state-building agenda when pronouncing the goal of "state-building for peace" (Rocha Menocal 2011, 1715).

Apart from the discussions between the "building"-discourses, there is a central flaw relatable to all of them: They are described to have a neo-imperial notion by transferring Western or even euro-centric visions on foreign countries (Fukuyama 2005, 131-132). Particularly, Richmond (2013, 130) declares them "failed by design" as he observes the whole policy process (planning, assessment, evaluation) headed by outsiders. This critical insight has contributed to the emergence of the "local ownership"-paradigm on the international agenda meaning the active participation and self-determination of local actors from the very beginning of any initiative (Krause 2010, 169). In practice, state-building efforts today are mostly endogenous, though they involve a considerable amount of external contribution (Sisk 2013, 7). Nevertheless, for some cases, it is doubted that these ambitions are of any success without constant exogenous support. Conrad Schetter (2005, 8-9) labelled these cases internationally administered quasi-protectorates – presenting Afghanistan as an example. Considering the environment in which state-building (or respectively peace-building or nation-building) efforts take place, local ownership has proven to be difficult to realise, starting from the very initial identification of the adequate local partners (Krause 2010, 169). This remark needs to be taken into account when analysing the suitability and sustainability of state-building measures as the pathway to stability, security and development.

The critical confrontation of the concepts has revealed that the different "building"-agendas employ distinct perspectives concerning similar and sometimes overlapping areas in conflict-affected environments (Grävingholt, Gänzle and Ziaja 2009, 1). All the same, the programmes are not mutually exclusive per se, but instead require a holistic approach necessary to match their actions for the benefit of their common goal of sustainable stability in a fragile context (ibid.). Such coordinated approaches are also called "whole-of-government" or "3D"-approaches to state-building as they consider all dimension of governance and the interconnectedness of policy issues (OECD 2009, 85). From an analytical perspective, this implies to be aware and to observe possible intersections between separated or intertwined "building"-agendas in their target region.

2.3. Study Focus: Security Sector Reform in State-Building

The review of the state-building concept, including insights from other "building"-discourses, has resulted in a critically assessed and adapted catalogue of practices today. Having said that, critical remarks and conceptions do neither automatically translate into a real-life change of practices nor automatically solve the issue they hint at. The continuous reflection and adaption of state-building on the international agenda testifies the acknowledgement of its own imperfection, but also the willingness to further improve (OECD 2008, 20). For instance, the OECD reviewed international engagement in fragile states under the subheading "Can't We Do Better?" (OECD 2011a). Yet both the implementation of state-building projects and their assessment have proven to be a challenge (Sisk 2013, 9). Answering the OECD's question requires a thorough assessment of state-building practices that aims at a better understanding of processes, shortcomings and the impact of such efforts. Due to the complexity of the agenda, the following case study concentrates exemplarily on an integral part of the state and state-building: the reconstruction of security.

Primarily, the re-establishment of security is pursued under the banner of security sector reform, although other activities apart from this agenda (e.g. concerning the education system, etc.) also add to security as a whole. As we have seen at the beginning of this chapter (in section 2.1.), security is emphasised as a central state function by state theory classics such as Thomas Hobbes, John Locke or Charles Tilly. Security is at the core of the state's legitimacy, hence the "social contract" that ties the state and its people to mutual rights and obligations (Hirschmann 2016, 20-21). In essence, security provides the basis for the mere survival of a state and its people (Stütz 2008, 178). Correspondingly, security takes a special role in state-building as the sine qua non of an effective state (Caplan 2005, 45). Krause (2010, 158) underlines that without security, there is no successful state-building. Security is thus both a catalyser and a goal of state-building. Beyond that, security is a critical precondition of development as it creates the basis for secure livelihoods and the environment for economic investments (Sisk 2013, 103). This security-development nexus has been recognised by international organisations resulting in a revised security concept tying individual to state security (OECD 2008, 13).

After the 9/11 attacks, the debate about state-building and fragility has intensified, accompanied by a "securitization" of international politics (Debiel and Rinck 2017, 405). This resulted into an expansion of the original security term and the incorporation of previously unrelated issues, e.g. economy, health, environment, into the security agenda. Critics of the "securitization"-shift argue it leads to a militarisation of originally non-military subjects while diluting the clout in core areas of security (Hänggi 2010, 78-79). The expansion of the security term already commenced in 1994, when the United Nation Development Program (UNDP) presented a new concept of human security in its Human Development Report (UNDP 1994, 3). In general, human security means the freedom from threats affecting individuals. It covers a plethora of dangers ranging from crimes, to economic disruptions, to environmental threats (ibid.). This people-centred concept spurred the shift of attention in international security-building practices towards state-society relations intensifying in the 2000s, but entailing a more negative connotation with the wording of "securitization".

The broadening of the security term introduced a new perspective into SSR by stressing the interconnections between traditional state security agents such as the military or the police and civilian organisations including the parliament, the jurisdiction, the media, et cetera (Hänggi 2010, 80-83). Underscoring the broad notion of this agenda, the OECD even refers to SSR as "security system reform"[18] (OECD 2008, 5). Similarly, so called post-liberal[19] research criticised state-centric approaches as concentrating solely on the reconstruction of state capabilities while neglecting the local context of everyday practices (ibid., 409-410). The specific relation between civil society and the state in everyday life constitutes an important factor of state-building and state performance which has been recognised on an international level as expressed by the concept of human security. In 2008, the UN Secretary-General even stated regarding the prospects of SSR: "The participation of non-State actors such as civil society organizations and the media is critical" (United Nations 2008, para. 41).

While the scope of security has broadened, a contrary observation has been made concerning the comprehensiveness of state-building methods. According to this, "securitization" translated into a narrower framework of actions in terms of a pragmatic reduction of the state to its core security institutions during international interventions such as in Afghanistan (Debiel and Rinck 2017, 407-408). Whereas international engagement in state-building

---

18 As the OECD defines its SSR-concept as follows: "The terms ['security system reform' and 'SSR'] also denote activities sometimes referred to by international actors as 'security sector reform', 'security and justice sector reform' and 'rule of law'" (OECD 2008, 5).

19 "Post-liberals" criticise that state-building approaches have been guided by a liberal Weberian (Western) model emphasising democracy and participation, and misplacing their attention to a timely drop-out in the event of elections as the end of international engagement (Sisk 2013, 66).

clearly exceeds the mere reconstruction of security forces, it has certainly become a significant "centre of gravity" as Hammes (2015, 277) puts it. Associated with the capability to manage security was – and still is – an exit strategy for international engagement (ibid.). The UN recognises that progress in security is essentially linked to the restoration of self-administration, hence the local autonomy of the states in question – explaining the special emphasis of state-builders on this issue (Sisk 2013, 80). However, the accentuation of a timely drop out can be viewed critically considering the long-term nature of SSR highlighted by Hänggi (2010, 97).

With regard to our case study, the diverging observations and critical remarks concerning the impact of "securitization", as well as political planning, the inclusion of local forces, the civil society and historical structures must be taken into account. These points need to be observed against the backdrop that the security sector also provides instruments of oppression and violence to decision makers in a state (Hänggi 2010, 77). In conflict affected environments like Afghanistan, security actors, such as the police or the military, have a legacy of abusive practice which needs to be critically assessed and dealt with in SSR (Mayer-Rieckh 2013, 5-7). Thus, the efforts to reappraise the past, to strengthen democratic accountability and legitimacy, and to orientate at the people's needs are critical for the success of the agenda. This corresponds with the broadly accepted intended trajectory of SSR as defined by the UN and the OECD (ibid., 8-9).

Concentrating on security as our access point for analysis does not imply an overemphasis of the sole contribution of SSR, nor neglect the importance of other areas (e.g. economic support or constitution making) for sustainable and peaceful development. Quite the contrary, focusing on SSR allows observing the complex relations within international state-building, as well as its intersections with the related peace-building and nation-building approaches. Security represents a frequently highlighted essential core of and for the state. Reviewing its understanding in international politics has revealed significant parallels to the state-building debate itself. In particular, the emphasis on state-society relations, the complexity and broadening of the task as well as scepticism towards international engagement illustrate analogous discussion patterns to the broader state-building discourse. As an access for analysis, the exploration of security reconstruction in the course of SSR sheds light on a groundwork for international engagement and development prospects in the wide array of state-building activities.

2.4. Stopover: The Knowns and Unknowns of State-Building

This chapter examined the theoretical foundations of state (re-)construction that shape international engagement in state-building. These findings guide the following chapters and are necessary to understand the diverging interpretations about the state, its basic functions and logics of action that drive international endeavours. Starting with an overview of state theory, the imperative for security became apparent, along with the main obstacle of research in this area: the complex, multi-layered and multi-faceted nature of tasks (Sisk 2013, 96). Additionally, as the first part of this chapter has shown, defining the concept of the state revealed a certain definitional fuzziness which is consequently conveyed to the concept of state-building. There is neither a universally accepted definition of the state nor of state-building. By contrast, the different lines of debate rest on a basic consensus that a minimum degree of security is an indispensable condition for any progress in war-affected territories (World Bank 2012, 25). Therefore, choosing the framework of security sector reconstruction within international state-building efforts exemplifies the possibilities and limits of such actions while enabling the analysis of a complex field regarding a key aspect of debate.

The review of theories unveiled that in any case international engagement in foreign territories is confronted with an imperialist and Eurocentric appeal (Fukuyama 2005, 131-132). State-building approaches have abandoned the track of enforcing the external design of a Western-style nation state on paper, favouring today context-sensitive, adaptive and locally owned processes (Grävingholt, Gänzle and Ziaja 2009, 3). The implementation of this in everyday practice has proven to be difficult starting with the identification of and cooperation with suitable local partners (Krause 2010, 169). From a donor perspective, this is related to the difficulty to balance the long-term character of this endeavour with internal (e.g. high costs) and external (e.g. hostility from the local populace) pressures for early withdrawal (Sisk 2013, 85). These areas of tension need to be taken into consideration when analysing SSR-initiatives. Furthermore, normative motifs fundamentally guide intervention, hence their impact on programmes lead by different donors need to be examined.

Outlining the state-building debate has demonstrated profound scepticism towards the general prospects of the whole agenda based on the negative track record of such missions plus the historical roots of state evolution (Debiel and Rinck 2017, 404). Evidence has shown that the improvement of institutional capacities is a slow process that is accompanied by continual revisions and refinement of state-building methods and concepts (World Bank 2011, 10, OECD 2011a). The recognition of growing state-fragility and internal conflicts accelerated the focus on state-building measures, as well as their impact assessments calling for process tracking and comparative research within and between countries targeted by state-building (Debiel and Rinck 2017, 405 & 412).

Literature about state-building or SSR in Afghanistan mostly concentrates either on a certain national perspective (e.g. Wieker 2012 on Germany) or a specific security provider such as the military or the police (e.g. Wilder 2007 on the later). Only few compare different parts of SSR, but these studies are either outdated (e.g. Sedra 2006) or do not integrate their analysis into the state-building and SSR discourse (e.g. Giustozzi 2016, Hammes 2015).[20] Other studies have managed to incorporate many aspects of SSR and state building, but then again do not focus on Afghanistan (e.g. Mayer-Rieckh 2013). Therefore, the current state of literature already answers numerous questions about the evolution and (externally addressed) modelling of a state, security and its function, the reconstruction of state capabilities, and – or related to – Afghanistan. Hardly anyone merges the interrelated aspects of these subjects into one comparative and up-to-date study. Yet, the termination of ISAF in December 2014 and the launch of its follow-up mission Resolute Support calls for an integrated study of security sector reconstruction and its contribution to the overall state-building process of the country. This research fills that gap by providing a comparative analysis of SSR projects as part of international state-building. The study incorporates both the historic development and the most recent findings concerning Afghanistan in order to derive a critical assessment of the SSR agenda and present policy implications for future engagement. Since the review of state-building and SSR theory uncovered the complexity of the issue, the next chapter is devoted to develop a methodological framework for the case study integrating the critical remarks presented above.

20 Please note that Hammes (2015) provides a US-focused analysis of the reform processes and future policy options – referring to the former observation of nationally-coloured studies.

3. Developing a Methodological Framework for Analysis

The study aims to elucidate the contribution of security sector reconstruction to state-building in Afghanistan. Under examination is therefore the specific security sector in the country in order to identify the impact and prospects of – and on – state-building efforts. In doing so, the study follows the OECD's call for the development of an "in-depth understanding of SSR processes and sector-specific reform needs" (OECD 2008, 23) in order to inform and review international actions. Due to the complexity of the agenda, this requires the creation of a methodological framework on how to analyse and compare such processes in a specific context like Afghanistan. With regard to the theoretical foundations presented, this chapter discusses the methodological considerations to SSR assessment. Subsequently, a conceptual framework is developed to facilitate the case study's feasibility and comparability for a set of selected evaluation criteria.

3.1. A Closer Look at Methodological Implications

In social sciences, the first step of diving into research is to decide for a qualitative, quantitative or mixed-method approach depending on the research question. In order to assess the contribution of SSR to state-building in Afghanistan, a sole quantitative approach does not fit the need to assess the historic context of the country, the legacy and perceptions of the institutions in question, and the SSR-approach applied by the different lead nations. These points are highlighted by state-building theories as described in chapter 2.

The general progress of SSR in Afghanistan, or public perceptions towards institutions are measurable with a quantitative study. This requires a solid data foundation (including a baseline measure) as well as carrying out surveys with Afghan people in the field. Such data is, however, hardly available for conflict-affected areas. Barton (2010) presents that this is a manageable challenge, yet the studies presented for Afghanistan are largely overrated considering the recent developments. Moreover, the availability and quality of data in conflict-torn countries is oftentimes incomplete as data collection mechanisms fall short in times of combat and even beyond (OECD 2008, 73-74). For example, in Afghanistan the latest census data dates back to 1979 and was described as unreliable at that time (Barton 2010, 26). On the other hand, there is broadly available literature published by Afghanistan experts (such as Antonio Giustozzi), governmental bodies, and non-governmental organisations or research institutions focusing on Afghanistan (as the AREU). Hence, certain statistics are collected and analysed, but they still require careful handling and critical reflection. On this account, the study makes use of an extensive qualitative document analysis as its primary approach for assessing the contribution of SSR to state-building in Afghanistan. At the same time, the analysis is complemented – in other words triangulated – by existing quantitative research for gauging the progress of SSR and state-building (e.g. capability ratings). In a broader view, the Bertelsmann Transformation Index provides aggregated data on state transformation complemented by country profiles (Bertelsmann Stiftung 2016).

As an external evaluation of a reform agenda, the study is subjected to certain advantages and limitations. First, the outside evaluation of SSR in Afghanistan is not affected by regulatory restrictions. Additionally, the analysis is not linked to any of the programmes yielding politically independent results (OECD 2011b, 46-47). On the other hand, this external analysis cannot draw on first-hand experiences or self-conducted field research. Hence, the study relies on observations and findings published by others. In order to mitigate this drawback, the sources of information are transparently reported.

Given the complexity of the agenda, it is not possible to cover all aspects and cross-sections of SSR and state-building. To moderate the risk of omitting central contextual information, the analysis orientates at analysis guidelines provided by the OECD's Handbook on Security System Reform (2008, 2011b). The guidebook presents a theoretical and practical footing for security sector reconstruction and evaluation. It evaluates experiences from former state-building approaches and presents guidelines for assessing the past, current and future SSR activities. For the purpose of this study, the handbook presents methodological guidance for conducting SSR assessments including analytical categories, evaluation criteria and exemplary questions (OECD 2008, 41-57, 241-242). In 2011, the assessment of SSR activities has been updated and published in an extended manual for monitoring and evaluation (OECD 2011b). With this, the OECD DAC serves as a central point of reference in the international development and state-building community (Schmidt 2013, 285). This does not automatically guarantee a sound analysis, but it enhances reproducibility and transparency with regard to the research procedure. It is, however, important to acknowledge inductive fallacies concerning the transferability of results, i.e. it is hardly possible to conclude from the particular to the general (Blatter, Janning and Wagemann 2007, 185). Yet, the single case analysis of SSR in Afghanistan does not aim at the generalisability of country-specific findings (e.g. the historical or social context), but at a thorough comprehension of the processes studied. This in turn adds to the general SSR and state-building debate beyond Afghanistan and facilitates future research.

The preceding explanations illustrated that the research method combines inductive and deductive approaches. The basic conception of the study is thus related to the conceptual framework analysis of policy research (Blatter, Janning and Wagemann 2007, 30). Following its eclectic logic, a set of evaluation criteria, categories and guidelines serve as our analytical framework (ibid.). Designing this framework is rather based on an inductive approach; its application on a deductive logic. The explanatory as well as exploratory character of the study reflects the complexity of SSR and the need to establish comparable theory-based analysis. However, this requires in a next step to clearly set out the research focus, the evaluation criteria, and resulting steps of analysis.

3.2. Developing a Conceptual Framework for SSR Impact

For developing the conceptual approach to SSR assessment, it is necessary to specify the research objects of the study. While acknowledging the complex interdependencies within the security system of a country, the evaluation concentrates on two major suppliers of state security: the police and the military. These two institutions have been selected because they are highlighted as core providers of state and citizen security, e.g. by Sisk (2013, 87) or Hänggi (2010, 87). Furthermore, the police and the military are two critical bodies at the top of international reform agendas when it comes to regional stabilization or transformation in the wake of war (Sisk 2010, 70). The selection of the two research objects serves heuristic considerations as it allows for a focused study within a convoluted field. At the same time, the sector-specific assessment enables the observation of intersections to the aforementioned multiple security or development related features and actors, especially the involvement of the local civil society.[21]

Moreover, the approach facilitates a comparison between two related reconstruction agendas in the same regional context, but (originally set up to be) led by different stakeholders. In Afghanistan, the United States headed the military reconstruction, whereas Germany took the lead for police reform (Hammes 2015, 279). The basis of different lead nations facilitates the juxtaposition of chosen strategies, priorities, programming and normative frameworks. It also takes into account critical remarks to state-building such as the impact of foreign engagement – more explicitly, the unintended consequences on various sectors (Sisk 2013, 100). While the police and the military constitute two distinct bodies including their very own legal framework and reform needs, a comparison of the reform activities promotes an understanding of common problems and objectives (OECD 2008, 16). This meets the claims of forging a more integrative approach to SSR and its assessment without ignoring context-specific particularities.

Up to this point, the main challenge of SSR and state-building assessment has been emphasised a few times: its complexity. In order to examine the developments in Afghanistan since 2001, it is necessary to divide the reform agendas into manageable units that comprise the impact of SSR activities on state-building in the country. For evaluating the development programmes, the OECD DAC established five standard assessment criteria in 1991: relevance, effectiveness, efficiency, impact and sustainability (OECD 2008, 242). With the 2011-update of the handbook, they have been supplemented and expanded to eight criteria for SSR evaluation. The committee included ownership to sustainability in recognition of its role for the long-term success of measures (OECD 2011b, 49). Furthermore, they added coherence, coordination and consistency with values with respect to the manifold and interconnected SSR activities in target countries (ibid., 48-49). In the international community, the standard criteria are regularly applied for reviewing assistance programmes. They are used, among others, by the United States Agency for International Development (USAID; see Purcell, et al. 2016), the German Corporation for International Cooperation (Deutsche Gesellschaft für Internationale Zusammenarbeit (GIZ) GmbH 2015), or the Kreditanstalt für Wiederaufbau (KfW 2017). Thus, these criteria provide an applicable and internationally comparable framework for the assessment of military and police reform in Afghanistan. In the following,

21 See section 2.3

Table 1 summarises the eight evaluation categories as an overview of our assessment scheme.

	Evaluation Criteria	Definition in the Context of SSR	Points of Consideration
1	**Relevance / Appropriateness**	▪ The extent to which the SSR activity is suited to the priorities and policies of the target group, recipient and donor	▪ Addressing main security threats and needs of the state and the citizens ▪ Based on up-to-date context assessment ▪ Consistent with domestic system ▪ Technically adequate solution ▪ Balance of long-term and immediate / short-term considerations ▪ Inclusion of non-state actors / mechanisms ▪ Responsive and adaptive to changing circumstances ▪ Consistent with donor policies and priorities
2	**Effectiveness**	▪ The extent to which the SSR programme achieved its objective	▪ Match with intended outputs, purpose and goal ▪ Changes resulted from international intervention or other factors ▪ Reasons for the results (delivery or non-delivery of specified objectives) ▪ Recommendations or options to make intervention more effective
3	**Efficiency**	▪ The extent to which outputs – qualitative and quantitative - of the SSR initiative have been produced by the least costly inputs in order to achieve the desired results	▪ Efficiency aspects taken into account ▪ Measures during planning and implementation to ensure efficient use of resources ▪ Outputs efficiently delivered (options to reduce resources without losing quality and quantity of outputs; to increase output with the same amount of resources) ▪ Different type of intervention more efficient in terms of costs but with same results ▪ Was a worthwhile intervention given possible alternative uses of the resources

4	**Impact**	▪ The positive and negative changes produced by SSR, directly or indirectly, intended or unintended	▪ Effects of the intervention on people and institutions (intended/unintended; positive/ negative) ▪ Effect on well-being of different groups (women, men, boys, girls, etc.) ▪ Perception of the effects of the intervention by insiders / affected people ▪ Strengthening of institutions (capacity, accountability) ▪ Development and improvement of relevant policies due to the intervention ▪ Identification and measurement of changes ▪ Attribution of changes to intervention
5	**Sustainability & ownership**	▪ A measure of whether the benefits of SSR are likely to continue after donor funding has been withdrawn with special emphasis on the involvement of locals	▪ Access to justice and security over longer term by the population (creation of processes, structures and institutions) ▪ Human & institutional capacity ▪ Consistency between donor's priorities and domestic effective demands / needs ▪ Support by local institutions ▪ (Well) integration into local social and cultural conditions ▪ Management and leadership of reforms by locals ▪ Participation of partner country stakeholders in the planning and implementation of the intervention ▪ Appropriateness of goods, services and technologies provided appropriate to the economic, educational and cultural conditions in the partner country ▪ Maintenance of benefits after withdrawal ▪ Credible exit strategy envisaged or in place
6	**Coherence**	▪ Whether the support and initiatives of	▪ Cooperation within individual donor governments (or between if one programme) ▪ "Whole-of-government" mechanisms in place to support SSR

		different international actors and departments are operating together in a coherent and strategic fashion	▪ Collision (tensions) or reconciliation of donor priorities: "hard" security issues (e.g. counter-terrorism) versus development-style SSR objectives
7	**Coordination / Linkages**	▪ The extent to which the SSR activity incorporates and promotes the coordination between different parts of the security system and government strategies in the country	▪ Steps / Measures to forge strategic engagement across the security system on different levels ▪ Forge of links between different programmes, frameworks, plans and operations (peacebuilding, development, recovery, poverty reduction, gender equality, etc.) ▪ Consistency and complementarity with activities supported by different donor organisations
8	**Consistency with values**	▪ The extent to which the SSR programme has promoted key principles and values in security governance (e.g. democratic governance, respect for human rights, respect for the rule of law, transparency, accountability)	▪ Promotion of norms of good and democratic governance, respect for human rights and the rule of law ▪ Intervention designed and carried out in accordance with basic governance principles of transparency and accountability ▪ Promotion of equitable access to justice and security for populations

Table 1: SSR Evaluation Criteria (Source: Adaption based on OECD 2008, 241-242, 2011b, 48-50)

This catalogue of evaluation criteria facilitates the analysis by providing a limited, albeit wide-ranging set of critical dimensions. Reviewing the eight categories, they cover the essential aspects of state-building and SSR programmes which have been outlined in the theoretical sections 2.2 and 2.3. Yet, it has to be acknowledged that these criteria overlap in some aspects. For example, effectiveness enquires the achievements of programme objectives, though this could also be incorporated under "impact". This category observes, in a broader sense, the changes occurred in relation to the reform initiative. Still, the criteria forge an adequate framework for reviewing reform activities which facilitates the comparison of such complex and diverse agendas.

For evaluating the reform activities with the eight categories, a conflict profile is crucial as a first step of the case study, provided in section 4.1. This revision is essential to provide basic insights to the underlying drivers of conflict, such as the social, political, regional and international roots of security threats (OECD 2008, 50). The conflict portrait lays the foundation for central assessment aspects. For example, the appropriateness of actions can only be gauged against country-specific circumstances. The conflict analysis further reveals conflict parties, leading stakeholders, and developments on the ground to which the security sector reform and actors are expected to adapt (Schnabel and Born 2011, 6). Moreover, it outlines the structures of the security system in the country, i.e. the main state and non-state provider of security which constitute central components of SSR according to the OECD (2008, 22).

As a second step, the case study examines separately the police and the military reform in the country since 2001 (section 4.2. and 4.3.). First, the analysis reviews reform activities to give a topic-based overview. That includes the entry point of reform, key plans and measures, actors, and developments. Then, the eight evaluation criteria appraise the particular reform agenda, especially in view of external assistance. With this, main reform achievements, failures, challenges, and options, hence lessons learned from the engagement are concluded.

The study does not list in detail each and every activity of the military and police reform in the country as it should provide a condensed assessment of the overall process.[22] The main focus will be laid on thematically structuring the advisory efforts which facilitates the application of the evaluation criteria. For this purpose, the categories for reconstruction are graded by a

[22] Such a detailed overview including the broad historical context has already been compiled in the publications of Giustozzi and Isaqzadeh (2013) concerning the police, and Giustozzi (2015) for the army of Afghanistan.

model the KfW uses in its ex post evaluation reports (e.g. in KfW 2015). The KfW applies a six-point rating scale to the projects ranging from "very good" results (level 1) to no impact of or a deteriorated situation caused by the project (level 6). For "sustainability", however, the bank introduces a four-point scale ranging from "very good" to "inadequate sustainability" (KfW 2015, 7). This rating system presents a rather qualitative assessment as it employs a nominal scale without clear benchmarks. On the plus side, it provides a useful rating tool in order to assess the reform agenda and its outcomes. The KfW (2017) insufficiently explains the application of a separate scale for sustainability.[23] The special scale complicates the comparison of results and calculating an average score for a reform. The KfW does not adjust the different scales in this calculation, but accepts the different weight for the four-point sustainability scale. Despite this complication, the paper follows the KfW's approach for the sake of comparability to its assessments and the limited scope to develop a diverging rating scheme. On the positive side, the scale-based system enables a graphical presentation of the ratings, thus facilitating the comparison of results – with the limitation of the four-point scale to be included in the figure. In order to give an overview of the rating scale applied to the reform process, table 2 summarises the KfWs evaluation scale.

Rating	Rating Description	Four-Point Scale for Sustainability
Level 1	Very good result that clearly exceeds expectations	Very good sustainability: The developmental efficacy of the project (positive to date) is very likely to continue undiminished or even increase.
Level 2	Good result fully in line with expectations and without any significant shortcomings	Good sustainability: The developmental efficacy of the project (positive to date) is very likely to decline only minimally but remain positive overall. (This is what can normally be expected).
Level 3	Satisfactory result – project falls short of expectations but the positive results dominate	Satisfactory sustainability: The developmental efficacy of the project (positive to date) is very likely to decline significantly but remain positive overall. This rating is also assigned if the sustainability of a project is considered inadequate up to the time of the ex post

[23] The KfW states: „For the criterion of sustainability we only use a four-point scale, which mainly reflects the anticipated future trend (albeit with a certain degree of uncertainty). A score of 4 indicates 'insufficient sustainability'" (KfW 2017). This description, however, does not provide an explanation for abandoning the six-point rating for sustainability.

		evaluation but is very likely to evolve positively so that the project will ultimately achieve positive developmental efficacy.
Level 4	Unsatisfactory result – significantly below expectations with negative results dominating despite discernible positive results	Inadequate sustainability: The developmental efficacy of the project is inadequate up to the time of the ex post evaluation and is very unlikely to improve. This rating is also assigned if the sustainability that has been positively evaluated to date is very likely to deteriorate severely and no longer meet the level 3 criteria.
Level 5	Clearly inadequate result – despite some positive partial results, the negative results clearly dominate	
Level 6	The project has no impact or the situation has actually deteriorated	

Table 2: Rating Levels for Project Evaluation (Source: Adaption based on KfW 2015, 7)

In a third step, these assessments are merged for estimating their impact on the overarching state-building venture in Afghanistan (section 4.4). Having said that, there is no "end state" of statehood to measure a state's development against as all states are subject to constant change (Sisk 2010, 58). State performance research is incorporated to assess the functionality of state institutions, for example by the Bertelsmann Transformation Index (Bertelsmann Stiftung 2016). Such data adds to the overall assessment of state-building activities in a country. Still, it is necessary to clarify the key dimensions for impact assessment. Sisk (2013, 53) suggests four categories: autonomy, authority, legitimacy and capacity. Autonomy describes the freedom from foreign control or narrow partisan interests. Authority means the sole and rightful use of coercive power. Legitimacy in the sense of Jellinek[24] refers to the internal and external perception of the right to rule. The concept of capacity captures the state's ability to plan and provide certain services to its citizens – e.g. security and justice (ibid.). The World Bank (2012, 26) presents a similar set of dimensions in its tool-kit for state-building guidance. In contrast to Sisk, however, the autonomy dimension is not separately listed. It is

[24] See section 2.1.1.

implicitly covered by the other three categories, particularly by state authority as it demands autonomy for making and implementing decisions on its own.[25] Therefore, the impact of SSR – with regard to military and police reform efforts – on state-building is gauged by appraising the three dimensions authority, legitimacy and capacity as suggested by the World Bank (2012, 26). Subsequently, the results of the case study and the methodological approach are discussed, reflected and concluded in the final chapter.

By this means, the analysis is of interest for stakeholders concerned, development workers and researchers, and even for the training personnel on the ground (OECD 2008, 25-26). Moreover, the study informs about the long-term nature of SSR, its limitations, and contemporary challenges to both political decision makers and the public. Analysing the foreign engagement in SSR in Afghanistan also enhances transparency and accountability in the donor countries. Eventually, the research approach and the answers presented aim to guide future investigations and international engagement.

---

25 Sisk (2013, 46) underscores that the aspects are oftentimes interconnected and sometimes even mutually reinforcing. He gives the example that the ability to govern in terms of authority is at times contingent on the consent of the ruled as an expression of legitimacy.

4. Case Study Afghanistan

The case study starts with the conflict portrait in section 4.1 including state-building policies. In a next step, the building-approaches are unravelled and graded in section 4.2 for the police, in 4.3 for the military. Section 4.4 merges the SSR results regarding the over-arching state-building project and concludes lessons learned. The final chapter 5 summarises the main results of the thesis and outlines its implications for research and state-building.

4.1. Conflict Portrait and State-Building Approach

The following conflict study examines the main context in Afghanistan to derive a common understanding of major security threats to which a security sector reforms is directed at. However, this portrait does not strive for completeness due to the limited scope of this paper in contrast to the vast extent of the conflict.[26] Additionally, it needs to be pointed out that the paper does not aim to provide a solution for the conflict, but to reveal some of its driving causes that affect SSR and state-building.

The roots of conflict can be traced back in time even before the foundation of the Afghan state itself. Nevertheless, this paper concentrates on the developments since 2001, as this year constitutes the beginning of the current conflict and subsequent international state-building efforts. The analysis still requires referring to certain episodes before this date in order to understand some contemporary challenges to SSR.

The Taliban ruled over the majority of the country since 1996, proclaiming the Islamic Emirate of Afghanistan. The Northern areas have been controlled by the so called Northern Alliance formed by former Defence Minister Ahmad Shah Massoud, the Uzbek warlord Abdul Rashid Dostum and

[26] For a comprehensive overview of the conflict history in Afghanistan, please refer to the writings of Tamim Ansary (2012) and Stephen Tanner (2012).

other leaders of many former anti-Soviet groups (Ansary 2012, 243). Notably, certain ethnic groups dominated the warring blocs. On the one side the predominantly Pashtun Taliban, on the other side the Northern Alliance consisting largely of Tajik, Uzbek and Hazara people. This internal war about ruling power raged in the country, though Pakistan and Saudi Arabia recognised the Taliban as the new government of the country (Schetter 2009). Pakistan is still considered as one of the main supporter of the Afghan Taliban which points at one international driver of the conflict (Ruttig 2015). Even the USA were interested in the Taliban at first. It was hoped that the fundamentalist but not perceived as anti-western regime would bring stabilization, disarm militias and former Mujahedeen forces, and contain Iran (Krüger 2014, 13-14). The U.S. government distanced itself politically from the Taliban regime in 1996, though this cannot be equated to active steps against them (Schetter 2009, 83). After the attacks on 11 September 2001, the Taliban refused to extradite the suspected mastermind of the attacks, al-Qaida leader Osama bin Laden, to the USA. They demanded evidence of his direct involvement, which the USA did not publicly offer (Krüger 2014, 39). As a reaction, the USA opened their "War against Terrorism" on 7 October 2001 with air strikes under the "Operation Enduring Freedom" (OEF). Meanwhile, the almost depleted Northern Alliance repulsed the Taliban on the ground. Within three months, the Taliban relinquished power and retreated to their last strongholds in the Pashtun tribal areas in the border region to Pakistan (Schetter 2009, 86). The Northern Alliance moved into Kabul and, according to Ansary (2012, 262), the people thought, the war was over.

At the same time, the international community already started at re-organizing government structures in Afghanistan for the future. While the original objectives following the 9/11 attacks have been to destroy al-Qaeda and overthrow the Taliban regime, the targets broadened after this first phase of military success (Grenier 2015, 8). On 5 December 2001, the Bonn Agreement was reached which laid the foundations of state-building and government reconstruction in Afghanistan. The conference's outcome was a four-phase plan that should establish key government structures within a mid-term period. In the first phase, a six-month interim government administered the country charged with organising a loya jirga, an assembly of all Afghan tribes. This grand assembly had the task to establish a transitional government and elect its leader to complete the second phase. The third phase foresaw a two-year transition period that should be dedicated to draft a new Afghan constitution. The fourth and last phase would then be completed with presidential and parliamentary election, thus the unfolding of Afghanistan into a parliamentary democracy (Ansary 2012, 267-268).

The plan was immediately turned into reality by appointing Hamid Karzai as provisional president. In order to establish a secure environment for the interim government, ISAF was created with an original size of up to 5000 forces. In 2002, Hamid Karzai was confirmed transitional president by an emergency loya jirga. By 2004, the constitutional loya jirga passed the new constitution based on a compromise of Islamic and democratic values. This includes, among others, the legal equality of women and men. In the same year, Hamid Karzai won the first presidential elections with 55.5 percent of all votes. In the following year on 18 September, parliamentary elections were held. They marked the end of the Bonn Agreement and were a full success on paper (Schetter 2009, 88-89).

However, there are flaws of the Bonn Agreement and its implementation that turned into drivers of conflict. The 2001 Bonn Conference did not invite Pashtuns of the rural south and southeast, although they constitute a considerable segment of Afghanistan's population.[27] It was feared that the Taliban, who had arisen from them, could revert to power incognito (Ansary 2012, 267-268). By excluding a significant part of the population from the negotiation table, the Agreement forfeited some legitimacy among those people.[28] Furthermore, the process reflects the fragmentation between the wealthy, more progressive urban areas of the north and the impoverished, more traditional rural tribal south (ibid.). It is also one reason for the polarization of the people in view of introducing human rights, democracy or the empowerment of women. According to Schetter (2009, 98), such changes were perceived as anti-Islamic and challenging the traditional order by large parts of the rural population.

Concerning the state structure, the Bonn Agreement established a centralized administration while disregarding the disparities between Afghan state bureaucracy and decentralized tribal governance (Ansary 2012, 269). Therefore, the introduction of such bureaucracy marked the institutionalisation of conflict lines in Afghanistan: between modernizing interests and subnational, patrimonial ones (Zimmerman 2015, 17). Despite the efforts to support the transitional government under Hamid Karzai, it remained weak and could hardly govern beyond Kabul, let alone in the distant rural areas. This resulted in a lack of territorial control, thus insufficient capacity to raise taxes or provide security (Schetter 2009, 90). Some observers like Otłowski

27 With approximately 12.5 million people, the Pashtuns constitute the largest ethnic group in Afghanistan (Krüger 2014, 305).

28 Even though Hamid Karzai is a Pasthun (Ansary 2012, 270).

(2014, 2-3) even argue that the Afghan government would not have survived a month without foreign support.

Looking closer at the achievements of each phase of the Bonn Agreement, the image of success receives further stains. The constitutional jirga was accused to consist of warlords and criminals (Ansary 2012, 273). The elections in this phase, but also the subsequent 2009 presidential elections are said to be rigged by widespread and systematic fraud (Zimmerman 2015, 20, Schetter 2009, 89).[29] The recruitment processes of the new government were characterized by patronage, nepotism, dominated by warlord-interests and personal networks – delegitimizing the government in the eyes of large parts of the population (Schetter 2009, 90).

The international coalition, on the other side, sharply increased its clout over time. Still, ISAF and the OEF remained two separate missions with specific operational goals – although their objectives are overlapping in some areas. The OEF focuses on counter-terrorism, while ISAF concentrates on the establishment of security by international presence and advisory programmes (ibid., 93). The OEF was based on a "coalition of the willing" under U.S. command. ISAF, on the other hand, was conducted on a multilateral basis – whereas the state-building approach was based on the "lead nation" concept. The December 2002 conference in Bonn established a five-pillar program to Afghanistan's reconstruction. According to this, Germany presided over the remodelling of the Afghan National Police (ANP), the U.S. over the Afghan National Army (ANA), the UK over counter-narcotics, Italy over the judicial reform, and Japan over DDR of former combatants (Porter 2015, 185).

The plan also anticipates the expansion of international engagement in Afghanistan. Mandated by the UN Security Council in October 2003 (UNSCR 1510), ISAF expanded its original operational area beyond Kabul (ibid., 186). Until October 2006, the mission stretched out over Afghanistan's full territory accompanied by an increase of foreign forces in the country (Krüger 2014, 49-50). Gradually, it became one of the largest and most complex advisory missions in history with tens of countries and numerous international organisations involved (Giustozzi and Kalinovsky 2016, 237). From 2009 to 2010, the number of international forces deployed in Afghanistan exceeded 100.000 and climbed up to almost 140.000 until 2012 (Rut-

29 The 2004 presidential elections are considered as a successful exception due to the high voter turnout, especially the participation of women. Still, the results and success of the elections are questionable in view of the high illiteracy rate in the country as well as limited campaigning of the candidates (Ansary 2012, 274-275).

tig 2016, 118, Krüger 2014, 157). Despite this high number, the involvement of almost 50 countries, plus diverging military cultures, hampered coordinated and consistent state-building (Hammes 2015, 279-280).

Though the international footprint in Afghanistan became heavier, radical forces recuperated. The border region to Pakistan served as a safe haven for the Taliban, where they regained strength, recruited and trained new members. This hardly passable territory is termed "Talibanistan" – a name reflecting the absence of both the Pakistani and Afghani state in these tribal areas (Hirschmann 2016, 105). The Pakistani support of the Taliban undermines effective cooperation between the states in addition to the already strained bilateral relations. A hot-button issue remains that Afghanistan does not recognise the Durand Line of 1893, the Afghan-Pakistan border, which is purposely parting the Pashtun tribal areas (Schetter 2009, 95). Furthermore, due to the Cashmere conflict, Pakistan is highly interested in preventing a pro-Indian orientation of the Afghan government, which is said to be one reason for their support of the Afghan Taliban (Ruttig 2015). Hirschmann (2016, 138) even states, there is no solution to the intra-Afghanistan conflict without managing the regional challenge of Pakistan.

Already in 2003, security started declining when the recovered Taliban went on the offensive. (Hammes 2015, 282). While they were outnumbered and outgunned by international forces, the Taliban enjoy the strategic advantage of local knowledge and the population's support. Hence, they are able to ambush, hide among and recruit from the locals (Krüger 2014, 59). Since the outbreak of war, the Taliban diversified beyond ethnic and social affiliations. They became a melting pot for those who are dissatisfied with the situation, especially for those against the "Western invaders". Incidents like the November 2008 bombing of the Wech Baghtu wedding party or American forces burning the Quran in February 2012 are just two examples of international misconduct that fuelled the Taliban's popularity and resentment against external forces (Ansary 2012, 331, Schetter 2009, 94-95). The burning of poppy fields for the sake of combating Afghanistan's drug economy means the loss of livelihood and lucrative revenues for the farmers. Signalled by high illiteracy rates[30] in the country, many peasants lack economic

[30] The BTI 2016 reports a total literacy rate of 31.7 percent in Afghanistan (17.6 percent for females and 45.5 percent for males). This rate is even higher in rural areas (Bertelsmann Stiftung 2016, 13, 20).

alternatives to the opium business. Anti-drug campaigns thus cause resentment that fuels the support for insurgent forces if they are not complemented by economic and educational support (Schetter 2009, 97-98).[31]

The killing of al-Qaida leader Osama bin Laden in 2011 was perceived a major victory in Western countries, especially in the United States. It also prompted the questioning of continued intervention and even calling for abandoning the mission (Grenier 2015, 60). Not even two months after bin Laden's death, U.S. President Barack Obama announced a drawback of U.S. forces in Afghanistan. However, the withdrawal of all combat forces until the end of 2014 had already been declared on 20 November 2010 (U.S. GAO 2013, 5). Despite that, Osama bin Laden's killing cannot be equated with an end of violence. Quite the contrary, his death sparked off a series of attacks demonstrating the insurgents' operational strength against the impression of their defeat (Ansary 2012, 330).

Next to the Taliban, there are other organisations willing to resort to violence, for example the Haqqani network and the IS-K. Still, the Taliban remain the most deadly network accounting for 43 percent of civilian casualties in 2016 according to UNAMA (2017, 7).[32] In 2015, the Taliban succeeded to conquer 23 of the 407 Afghan districts (Ruttig 2016, 117). By May 2017, 45 districts have been under control or influence by the insurgents – some more 119 districts are considered as contested areas where the actual situation was unclear (SIGAR 2017, 88). In their controlled districts, the Taliban have established their own administration including a shadow government, courts and a taxation system (Ruttig 2016, 118, Ansary 2012, 320). These developments do not only indicate a loss of government authority, but also that the war cannot be considered as ended but reigniting.

The rising number of casualties and the advance of insurgent and violent forces could not be prevented by the National Unity Government (NUG) under President Ashraf Ghani. Quite the opposite, the 2014 presidential elections have brought new turmoil in the country as they have been marked by mutual fraud allegations between the camps of Ghani and Abdullah (International Crisis Group 2017a, 5). The U.S. brokered a power sharing agreement between the opponents, but it entailed unclear competencies between the role of President Ashraf Ghani and the Chief Executive Abdullah

[31] The combat of Afghanistan's drug economy is complicated by the fact that not only the Taliban, but also government officials are involved in the opium business (Schetter 2009, 97).

[32] The report also notes an increasing impact of IS-K that accounted for 5 percent of all civilian casualties (899 out of 11418) in 2016, in contrast to 82 civilian casualties (out of 11034) in 2015. This sharp increase demonstrates its stronger foothold in the country and tactical relevance for international actions.

Abdullah causing ongoing tensions (Mattox 2015, 301). The NUG tries to revive the dialogue with the Taliban, but they refuse to negotiate with the "puppet government" of the West (Ruttig 2015). After their initial defeat, the Taliban sought for talks, but the USA turned down the request (Krüger 2014, 103). Renewed negotiations in 2010 failed by 2012, which was blamed on the misconduct of the Karzai administration. Due to a breach of confidentiality in 2015, the secret leaked that Taliban founder Muhammad Omar had died in 2013. The Taliban abandoned the negotiation table and have refused to return ever since (Ruttig 2015). In June 2017, President Ghani called for further peace talks. Again, the Taliban declined as they viewed it as a call to surrender (SIGAR 2017, 141).

On another front, the NUG has been more successful. In September 2016, it finalized a peace agreement with the Hezb-e Islami led by Gulbuddin Hekmatyar (ibid.). In former times, during the Soviet-Afghan War, the party fought against Soviet troops. Hekmatyar went into exile in Iran during the Taliban rule. Later, he strongly opposed the Karzai administration. He was perceived a permanent threat to ISAF and was put on the UN's terrorists list, while he maintained communication with the Afghan government (Krüger 2014, 112-113). The peace deal allowed Hekmatyar to return to Afghanistan and give a public speech in April 2017 as it also lifted the UN sanctions against him. This seems to be a Janus-faced decision: On the one hand, Hekmatyar called on the Taliban and other insurgents to lay down arms, which might open a new chance for peace. On the other hand, the peace contract was harshly criticized to create a culture of impunity and forget about Hekmatyar's victims. Additionally, the agreement included a list of 3.500 Hezb-e Islami members to join the Afghan security forces (SIGAR 2017, 141). The consequences of this decision remain to be seen, though one must be aware that Hekmatyar fought against the government and the "foreign crusaders" in the past (Schetter 2009, 94). Thus, the agreement bears the risk of great instability. The party's loyalty to the Afghan government and their willingness to cooperate with foreign advisors has yet to be proven which in particular applies to the prospective security forces.

In the run-up to ISAF's termination, the international alliance started to transfer the responsibility of security to the Afghans in some provinces in March 2011 and entered into the last phase of transition in June 2013 (Krüger 2014, 83). Though the Afghan government holds the full administrative responsibility, the Taliban-governed districts demonstrate that it is still far from having full authority. The Afghan government remains challenged by around 20 insurgent and terrorist networks in the country according to the U.S. Department of Defense (DOD 2017, 1). The completion of

ISAF did not mean the "end of war" and the Resolute Support mission staffed with around 13.000 forces proved its inability to stop the deterioration of security (Ruttig 2016, 118, Otłowski 2014, 2). As a result, the U.S. re-assessed the situation and demanded to send more NATO forces to Afghanistan. On 29 June 2017, U.S. Defence Minister Jim Mattis admitted at a press conference after a meeting of NATO defence ministers:

> "Looking back on it, it's pretty much a consensus that we may have pulled our troops out too rapidly, reduced the numbers a little too rapidly." (Stewart and Emmott 2017)

What Ruttig (2016, 118) calls a "retreat from the withdrawal" was then officially settled by the NATO defence ministers. Nevertheless, the planned increase of around 4.000 additional forces in Afghanistan stays behind the peak of more than 130.000 international troops – a number unable to end violence (Holland and Walcott 2017). In view of our research question, the following chapters reconstruct and assess the state-building efforts asking for the impact of SSR, which resulted in the statement of U.S. Defence Minister Jim Mattis and the deterioration of the security situation in the country.

For a better overview of the points considered in this conflict portrait, the following graphic (figure 1) sums up the roots of insecurity and conflict in Afghanistan that need to be considered for evaluation.[33] At the same time, each category provides a starting point for further research on the social, political, regional, and international aspects of conflict.

[33] Please note that some factors have to be left out due to heuristic purposes.

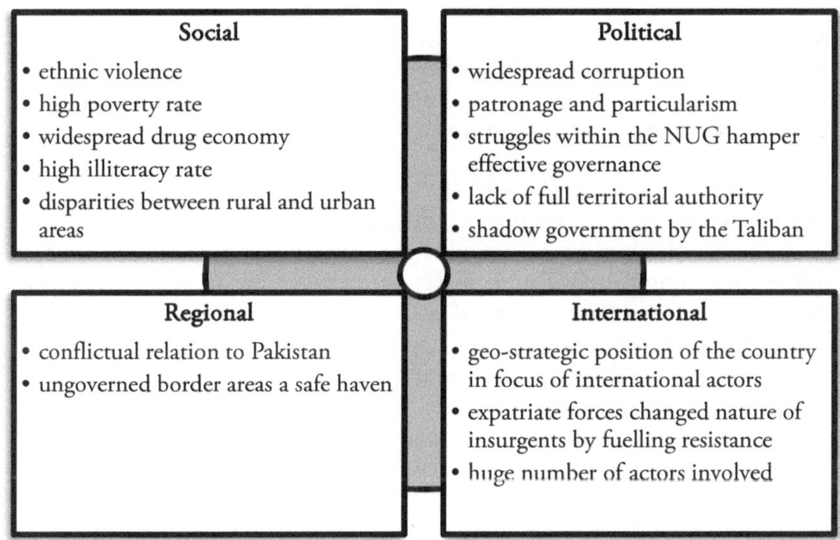

Figure 1: Security Risks in Afghanistan (Source: own figure)

4.2. The Afghan Police

In order to facilitate the evaluation of police reconstruction, the analysis is divided into three parts: First, the study examines the beginnings of police reform and their impact on the longer-term process (4.2.1). Secondly, the transition process is reviewed in combination with implications of the first part (4.2.2). In a third step, these findings are merged, supplemented and graded under the evaluation categories (4.2.3).

4.2.1. The Police Reform Agenda Starting from Scratch

As the entry point for the study on the reconstruction of the Afghan police serves its condition after the defeat of the Taliban. Under the Taliban, the police almost completely disintegrated as an institution. Instead, the Taliban executed their own basic system of policing that ignored bureaucratic rules and criminal procedure codes. The application of sharia law and draconian punishments had a deterrent effect resulting in a very low crime rate.[34] When the international community arrived to rebuild Afghanistan's institutions, it was a new year zero as there was no formal training procedure in place, almost no equipment and very few pre-Taliban policemen returning to duty. Hence, re-creating the police system from scratch was the starting point for engagement (Giustozzi and Isaqzadeh 2013, 34-37).

On the international side, the reconstruction of the police gained momentum at the Tokyo Conference in January 2002, when Germany assumed the lead nation role for rebuilding the Afghan National Police and subsequently organised a donor's conference in Berlin for the following month (Hammes 2015, 292). The original objective the donors agreed on was "to establish a multi-ethnic, sustainable, and countrywide 62,000-member professional police service that is fully committed to the rule of law" (U.S. GAO 2005, 8) without specifying any deadline. Germany's plan concentrated on the training of senior police and non-commissioned officers (NCOs) at the Kabul Police Academy. The German Police Project Office (GPPO) was established in 2002 tasked to conduct the advising in form of a 3-year course for senior police officers and a 1-year course for NCOs (Giustozzi and Kalinovsky 2016, 247, Hammes 2015, 292). Next to the German key role, ISAF established some small-scale Provincial Reconstruction Teams (PRTs) of different nationality to advise the police in their respected area, but their impact on the overall police reform was rather limited (Murray 2007, 111).

34 As far as one can judge from reports (e.g. by Giustozzi and Isaqzadeh 2013, 34-37) without the existence of a statistical office under the Taliban.

Meanwhile, the Afghans had already started filling the power vacuum resulting from the removal of the Taliban. While ISAF initially focused on the support of the transitional government in Kabul, the Northern Alliance faction leaders and other local warlords assumed control over provincial and district administration including the police. They filled the police posts with militia fighters with little or no police training or experience who gained the reputation of "robbers" among the population (Wilder 2007, 2-3). For the foreign advisors, these untrained combatants posed a challenge to build an effective, law-abiding police force obliged to serve their citizens and central government instead of factional affiliations. Further exacerbating the situation, the governmental institutions in charge, especially the Ministry of Interior (MOI) had also been apportioned to factional leaders (Hammes 2015, 291). As pointed out in section 2, this indicates the need for a whole-of-government-approach to state-building.

Yet the international approach to police reform was hardly interconnected. In 2003, the United States kicked in the Afghan police reconstruction and quickly surpassed the German contribution. Despite Germany being the lead nation, the United States had already outspent it by far in the early years of the project. Between 2002 and 2006, Germany contributed approximately $80 million to the mission, whereas the United States exceeded the $2-billion mark of spending for the ANP in the same period (Wilder 2007, 19). While there is quite a difference in the economic resources of Germany and the United States, the disparity of financial grants indicates a demise of the lead nation concept for police reform in Afghanistan (Giustozzi and Kalinovsky 2016, 241).

From an U.S. point of view, the German efforts to police reform were moving too slowly and neglecting the vast majority of the police: the patrolmen. Concerned about the upcoming 2004 presidential elections, the United States established a "train the trainers"-programme to enhance the police's capabilities. Before the elections, more than 20,000 police went through the training that was overseen by the U.S. Department of State's (DOS) Bureau of International Narcotics and Law Enforcement. The schedule consisted of an 8-week basic training course for new recruits or a 2-week course for veteran police. In addition, highway and border police underwent two more weeks of specialized training. For illiterate recruits, a shorter 4-week programme was designed. By 2005, Germany and the U.S. had trained more than 35.000 policemen and expected to achieve the goal of 62.000 by the end of the year (U.S. GAO 2005, 19-20).

However, the mere number of trained police deceives about inherent difficulties. The policing mission was fragmented into two separately running major programmes of the U.S. and Germany (in addition to several small-scale training activities of other countries) that were neither coordinated nor interlocked. The clash of the disparate visions of the ANP's role compounded this problem and was even of diplomatic friction (Murray 2011, 48-49). The Germans advocated a civilian law and order police force, while the United States favoured a paramilitary counter-insurgency role due to the precarious security situation (Hammes 2015, 300). The United States were internally divided on the issue, but the paramilitary vision prevailed, when the police training supervision shifted from the DOS to the Department of Defense (DOD) in 2005 (Murray 2011, 49). On the execution side, the militarization of the U.S. programme is underscored by the fact that the Combined Security Transition Command-Afghanistan (CSTC-A) assumed responsibility that also coordinated the U.S. efforts to re-model the Afghan army.[35] In contrast, when the European Union (EU) succeeded Germany's lead role of training and mentoring for senior police in 2007 with its European Union Police Mission (EUPOL), the civilian approach overruled internal disagreements in the EU. The parallel processes of police reform resulted in discordant training efforts and even overt bickering (Giustozzi and Kalinovsky 2016, 248, 285-286). Moreover, when the DOD took lead for the U.S. mission, it started training and advising senior police officials, compounding the coordination and execution problems between the dual agendas (Hammes 2015, 294).

The re-organisation of U.S. responsibility to the DOD did not solve its lack of human resources for conducting the training in Afghanistan. Already the DOS contracted with DynCorp Aerospace Technology "to train and equip the police, advise the Ministry of Interior, and provide infrastructure assistance" (U.S. GAO 2005, 8). Private contractors in Afghanistan like DynCorp have repeatedly been criticized for their lack of knowledge concerning the country and its people, their poor supervision and low quality of staff. These points have also been issued against police or military advisors, but the employment of private contractors remained particularly controversial (Giustozzi and Kalinovsky 2016, 255-258).

Taking a closer look at the ANP training, even more concerns were raised. First, concerning the quality of the programmes; second, about the quality of the recruits; third, about the sustainability of the results. Regarding the first point, the international parties were confronted with a system in shambles after a rapid intervention without much time to prepare for future governance. However, the programme designed for training the police was stuffed into a very short timeframe compared to common police training

35 See section 4.3 for more details.

curricula, e.g. in the United States. The limited teaching time was in fact even shorter considering that interpreters were usually required to translate the subject matter (Hammes 2015, 278, 293). The problem was somehow alleviated when the mission advanced over the years as education material was translated into Dari and other Afghan languages. Yet the language barrier between the majority of the trainers and their trainees remained given small number of foreign Dari-speaking personnel coupled with very few English-speaking (let alone literate) recruits.

This points to the relation between the first, the training programme, and the second concern, the quality of the recruits. As mentioned above, most policemen had not received any training before the international programme. Even worse, many had never seen a classroom before (Giustozzi and Kalinovsky 2016, 283). Although the aim was to establish an ethnically balanced, professional police, the vetting of recruits was of minor importance. Even in 2005, both the United States and Germany did not track the ethnicity of their trainees (U.S. GAO 2005, 21). Vetting in general was put in second place. Although in principle, every recruit had to be vetted before signing their contract, which required background checks and two individuals to vouch for the character of the prospective recruit, still in 2008, fewer than 5 percent failed to pass the vetting. The absence of a national crime database, the non-compliance of training centres to vetting procedures, the interference of politicians and officials in the process and their recommendation of protégés contributed to such small rejection rates (Giustozzi and Isaqzadeh 2013, 50). The little regard for who was being trained was already well known when the DOD took over and best described by the words of one provincial Chief of Police as "putting uniforms on thieves" (Wilder 2007, xi).

The effectiveness of the teaching method is questionable given the low literacy rate among the population in general and the police in particular – a problem that also concerns the military reform, as we will show. The U.S. programme designed a shorter training for illiterate recruits, but exact numbers about the actual number of recruits undergoing the different courses are not available as even the MOI denied for a long time the extent of the problem. In 2007, official statistics indicated a 30 percent-literacy level of the police (Giustozzi and Isaqzadeh 2013, 74-75). A sample literacy testing of the Afghan National Civil Order Police (ANCOP), the elite forces of the police supposed to be all literate, revealed a literacy rate of 5.3 percent. The total ANP literacy level was even estimated below that level by the SIGAR in 2011 (SIGAR 2011, 67-68). One reason for this below-average literacy rate was that men joined (due to low entrance requirements) who lacked economic alternatives precisely because of their low level of education (Wilder 2007, 30-31).

Still, literacy training remained an issue of second order up to 2010. Only since 2006, optional evening classes were established to provide literacy training, but in 2009, it was admitted that they failed to improve the situation significantly (Giustozzi and Isaqzadeh 2013, 75). As the literacy of police (and military) officials is directly related to their training prospects and, beyond that, to administrative issues, illiteracy compromises the chance for professionalization. Concerning the teaching of illiterate recruits, the standard PowerPoint-education by many trainers, especially private contractors, proved inadequate. This was further compounded by the fact that the material was often "cut and pasted" from previous deployments as in Kosovo and hardly adapted to the Afghan context (Giustozzi and Kalinovsky 2016, 263).

In 2009, the multi-national mission experienced a major re-structuring process, when the NATO Training Mission-Afghanistan (NTM-A) was established as part of ISAF tasked with police and military training. CSTC-A remained separate within the mission, while its commander dual-hatted the NTM-A. While the NTM-A strengthened the coalition and its coordination, it also added further complexity to its organisation (Hammes 2015, 296-297). Additionally, EUPOL ran its own training parallel to the NATO operation. Concerning the literacy programme, NTM-A established obligatory courses aiming to achieve 100 percent literacy at third grade level in the ANDSF by 2014 (SIGAR 2011, 67). Yet, it remains unclear whether the goal was achieved until today as the capabilities to track progress have been reduced resulting from the decrease of staff after ISAF's termination (Katzman and Thomas 2017, 33). A sample testing of ANP patrolmen carried out by the United Nations Educational, Scientific and Cultural Organization (UNESCO) Kabul indicates that the target was not met. The survey published in September 2016 revealed that "46% of the police patrol population cannot read, 32% cannot write, and 18% cannot solve numeracy problems" (UNESCO 2016, 25).

Concerning the third caveat, the sustainability of training results, the international advisors were confronted with a decline of training achievements already in the early years of the mission. For example, the 2005 GAO report notes that trained policemen had been returning to their duty stations where they were faced an unchanged environment of poorly trained colleagues loyal to local militias and their ethnicities. Surrendered to these structures, the trainees could not apply their newly gained skills, but resorted to old habits (U.S. GAO 2005, 22). In 2007, the recognition of the problem was answered by a major turnover of the U.S. approach launching the Focus District Development (FDD) plan. The FDD replaced previous programmes and was designed to eradicate the issue of defective home structures. For this purpose, all officers were withdrawn for two months from a district, trained and then redeployed under supervision of a police mentoring team. In their time of absence, ANCOP units, regarded as the most professional part of the police, temporarily executed the trainees' tasks. In theory, running through the programme provided professionalism to the whole district and the post-training on-the-job mentoring ensured that the knowledge gained was put into practice (Giustozzi and Kalinovsky 2016, 255). In contrast to previous U.S. programmes, where post-training mentoring was largely missing, FDD was a major improvement. Optimism about the new programme was expressed, but FDD came with a number of flaws (Hammes 2015, 292-294). It required per unit of 100 to 120 policemen twelve to eighteen trainers, thus it was very manpower intensive while such human resources were missing (Giustozzi and Isaqzadeh 2013, 50). Although with CSTC-A, and later NTM-A, the number of advisory personnel grew dramatically, the required numbers could not be achieved. In June 2008, less than 40 percent of the personnel required for the mentoring units was staffed. By January 2009, the mentoring teams could only cover quarter of the units envisaged (Giustozzi and Kalinovsky 2016, 256). That was particularly problematic as training results started decaying as soon as mentoring teams left.

Apart from that, the training duration of eight weeks was appraised too short to leave a mark on the recruits. In the run-up to the 2009-elections, the training time was scaled down to three weeks in order to cover as many districts as possible. This was criticized as overemphasising quantity and immediate results instead of striving for quality and sustainability. Before NTM-A took over in 2009, the training courses were regularly passing all trainees. Attendance was not even compulsory and reports state that many trainees only came to the first and last day of the course, which sheds a bad light on claimed successes. As a countermeasure, NTM-A tightened the training standards resulting in a 67 percent dropout rate among recruits in early 2010. Despite the enhanced basic training, even the 5 percent of trainees who failed the firearms tests were issued a weapon and sent to duty – disregarding their questionable eligibility in order to fill personnel targets. The FDD approach was abandoned in 2011 and replaced by an overhauled approach of basic training. Part of this was the innovative "Patrolmen Basic Program of Instruction" of March 2011, which was approved by both NTM-A and EUPOL, thus enhancing cross-mission coherence (Giustozzi and Isaqzadeh

2013, 50-51). Yet this joint approach was the only major cooperation between the separate NTM-A and EUPOL missions in police building.

The matter of sustainability of training results was and still is – as we anticipate issues of the next sections – highly affected by the attrition rate of the forces. Although attrition is a multicausal phenomenon, it hampers the future prospects of a force in matters of sustainability and professionalism. Just as other challenges, the high attrition rate of the ANP was recognised at an early stage, but could not be resolved until today. Reportedly, the ANP even suffers a higher desertion rate of about 2 percent a month than the Afghan army (Katzman and Thomas 2017, 35). The attrition rates differ between the districts and are much higher in provinces, where the insurgency is strong. In Helmand, a province called a Taliban stronghold, the overall attrition rate was 57 percent in 2008 to 2009. The rate is comprised of 12 percent resulting from casualties and 45 percent due to desertion or dismissal, often related to drug abuse (Giustozzi and Isaqzadeh 2013, 74). High attrition rates are compensated by positive recruitment rates. In this regard, it has to be kept in mind that new policemen need to be trained before deployment. Additionally, experiences and abilities of the leaving officers are lost to the force. This results in a disproportionally young and inexperienced police struggling with retaining their size and skills (DOD 2017, 71, 77).

In November 2009, a rise in police salaries to $260 per month in high combat areas stimulated an increase in recruitment and retention. In the preceding years, basic police pay was steadily increased from $16 per month in 2003 to $176 in 2010. In rural areas, the higher pay was enough to provide for a family in 2010. This does not apply to urban areas such as Kabul, where a lower middle class family needed approximately $600 a month. Eventually, the wage increase could only pause, not cease the high attrition rate. Furthermore, there was no evidence that higher salaries affected the level of corruption, which remains a great obstacle (Giustozzi and Isaqzadeh 2013, 73-74).

4.2.2. The Police under Transition to Full Responsibility

To stabilize the country for transition, it was necessary to establish a functional police system throughout Afghanistan. Remote areas have proven hard to reach leading to the creation of another pillar in the policing system: the Afghan Local Police (ALP). The idea was to enable local citizens to protect their communities against insurgent attacks and even conduct counterinsurgency missions by firm supervision of the MOI (SIGAR 2017, 103). Despite persistent reservations to support militias involved in felony crimes and human rights abuses, a series of programmes was tried since 2005 that finally consolidated under the Afghan Local Police programme in 2010. Each ALP fighter is selected by village elders, vetted by Afghan Intelligence[36], and trained by U.S. Special Operations Forces in order to build a stand-alone police force of up to 30,000 forces. In contrast to the ANP, the ALP is completely funded by the United States underlining its exceptional role in the Afghan security system (Katzman and Thomas 2017, 36).[37] When Special Forces lived among the ALP units, major improvements in professionalism have been noted and the ALP programme provided better security than its predecessors. As soon as the Special Forces left, the ALP units lacked supporting institutions (for salaries, equipment, fuel, spare parts, etc.) and even reverted to predatory practices (Hammes 2015, 298-299). ALP forces are accused of corruption, assault, rape, murder and other crimes reported by Human Rights Watch and the U.S. DOD (Katzman and Thomas 2017, 36). Many ALP fighters have been recruited from partisan militias, which raised concerns that they spur intertribal conflicts and might challenge the central government as their loyalty remains questionable (Hammes 2015, 299).

Clashes and disputes between local security units and governmental forces have been noted by the U.S. DOD, particularly, when the parties were of different ethnicities. Yet even ANP forces are reportedly involved in local factional or ethnic disputes as the police staff usually work in the communities they live in. Further compounding the problem, there are other local security forces, for example so called arbokai, which are formed without authorization and without supervision of any national institution. The toleration of informal security structures as well as their partial institutionalisation in form of the ALP undermined cross-sectoral reform efforts. Especially the DDR programme headed by Japan was partly reversed by arming instead of disarming local forces (Katzman and Thomas 2017, 35-37).

With the transition in mind, capability assessments gained particular importance. On the one hand, such assessments aim at ensuring transparency and accountability towards donor institutions and the international public. On the other hand, capability reports provide a useful tool to monitor, assess and interpret reform efforts. Under ISAF there had been periodic capability reviews. Once the international advisors left, so did the capacities for in-depth assessments. In the words of U.S. SIGAR John Sopko:

36 For a long time, the Afghans relied on international intelligence. While their intelligence capacities improved recently, intelligence analysis remains weak which questions the effectiveness of vetting ALP members (DOD 2017, 36).

37 The ANP is funded from different sources. A major source is the Law and Order Trust Fund Afghanistan (LOTFA) administered by the UNDP that pays ANP salaries and capacity building in the MOI until the Afghan government is able to completely fund and administer them itself (SIGAR 2017, 79).

"They [the RS advisers] simply do not have the presence to conduct such assessments. This is a serious concern because SIGAR and other U.S. oversight agencies have long questioned the reliability and accuracy of ANDSF assessments, at a time when those assessments had far more granularity than today." (Sopko 2016, 5)

SIGAR Sopko's quote confirms several problems concerning the assessments of capabilities that refer to both the ANP and the ANA. First, the rating definition changed over time hampering the comparability of results. The GAO 2009 report presented that 18 ANP units were categorized as "fully capable" to conduct missions on their own, 16 units as "capable with support" of international forces, 22 units as "partially capable" and 317 units not capable of conducting primary missions (U.S. GAO 2009, 19). In April 2010, the rating system was completely replaced with the Commander's Unit Assessment Tool (CUAT), but the rating levels changed four times until August 2011 (SIGAR 2014a, 6). A major change concerns the highest capability rating. The requirements for achieving the highest rating shave been significantly lowered by shifting from "independent", meaning full capability to plan and conduct missions, to "independent with advisors. The lowered standard resulted in higher ratings for the police: 39 ANP units achieved the top grade as of April 2012 (U.S. GAO 2012, 3-4). However, GAO highlights that the assessment tool was designed to rate counterinsurgency performance which omitted civil policing and other ANP responsibilities. Only by February 2012, these points have been included in the performance measure. Prior assessments are thus unusable to determine the capabilities of the ANP in key tasks of policing limiting insights and further questioning the appropriateness of the rating tool (ibid., 4).

The decline in international monitoring capabilities is most visible as the newest publicly available and detailed assessment of ANP (and ANA) capabilities is drawn from the SIGAR's 2014 report (SIGAR 2014a, 5). The results presented in figure 2 illustrate that the rating of ANP units differs significantly. While the capacities vary over time, the last reported 64 ANP units operating "independent with advisors" as of April to July 2013 even lag behind the July to October 2012-level of 71 units receiving the highest rating. A comparison between the results is further complicated by different number of ANP units varying between 366 and 517 without any reason. The decreasing monitoring capabilities are illustrated by the rising number of unassessed units. During the January to April 2012 period, only 24 out of 366 units were not assessed (around 6 percent). In the April to July 2013-period, more than 77 percent of all units (401 out of 517) remained unrated – exceeding by far the number of surveyed units thus decreasing the overall explanatory power and transparency of the results.

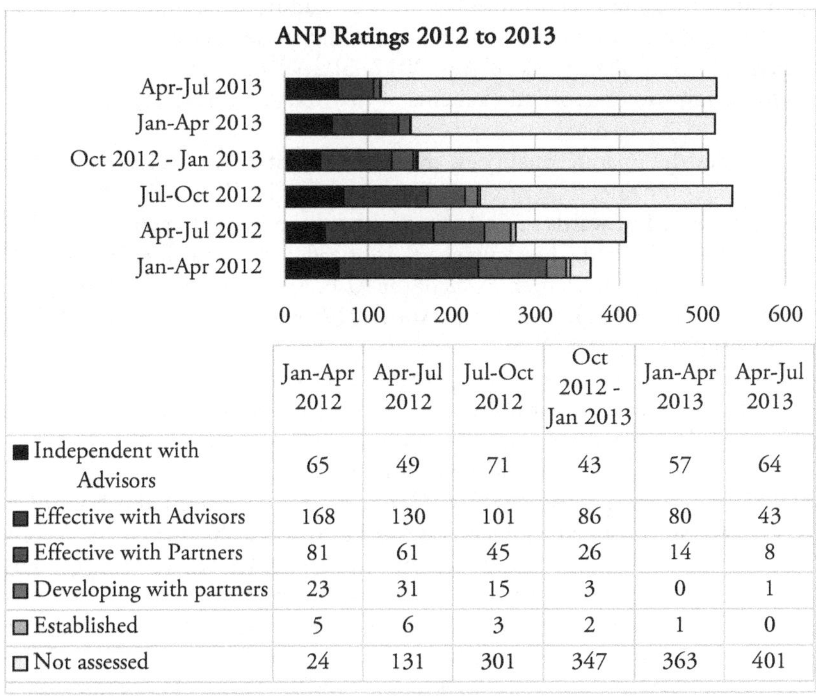

	Jan-Apr 2012	Apr-Jul 2012	Jul-Oct 2012	Oct 2012 - Jan 2013	Jan-Apr 2013	Apr-Jul 2013
Independent with Advisors	65	49	71	43	57	64
Effective with Advisors	168	130	101	86	80	43
Effective with Partners	81	61	45	26	14	8
Developing with partners	23	31	15	3	0	1
Established	5	6	3	2	1	0
Not assessed	24	131	301	347	363	401

Figure 2: ANP Ratings 2012-2013 (Source: own figure, data provided by SIGAR 2014a, 5)

Despite the questionable quality of the assessment, it was obvious that in view of the scheduled end of the transition period and ISAF in 2014, there was only a "narrow window of opportunity" to fully develop the ANP's capabilities[38] and ensure systematic oversight (SIGAR 2014a, 11). Yet the true capabilities of the police have to be questioned as the rating system itself created disincentives for the units to achieve top marks. As soon as units were rated accordingly, mentors and resources have been withdrawn entirely. Similarly, support for top rated ANA units was minimized and re-focused for lower-rating units. This was repeatedly stressed a major reason for backsliding in performance. Additionally, the rating system created incentives for CSTC-A staff to embellish the results: It was a self-assessment and training

[38] This also applies to the ANA's capacities as described in section 4.3.2 below.

results were potentially related to the career of the advisors in charge (Giustozzi and Isaqzadeh 2013, 53, 76). Therefore, during transition, security responsibility was transferred to ANP units of questionable capabilities while oversight abilities were steadily decreasing. Current detailed capability assessments are not available. As of July 2017, SIGAR only reported that force readiness improved across all elements of the ANA and ANP (SIGAR 2017, 82).

Besides the opaque quality of the ANP, quantitative achievements too remain questionable. The target end-strength for both the ANP and ANA has been revised upwards several times, although original targets had probably not been reached. The current authorized target size for the ANP is 157,000 including all elements except the ALP. According to the DOD 2017 report, this target was not met as of April 2017 as the ANP counted 148,710 personnel (DOD 2017, 76-77). The "exact police force level has always been quite a mystery" as Giustozzi and Isaqzadeh (2013, 74) point out. Estimates concerning the number of police in service vary significantly. In 2007, the personnel charts reported 75,400 policemen, whereas UNAMA estimated a true number of 39,500. While the personnel charts in 2010 noted 122,000, EUPOL's estimates reported 85,000 serving ANP (Giustozzi and Isaqzadeh 2013, 74). Since December 2014, it has been increasingly tried to address the problem by introducing the Afghanistan Human Resources Management System (AHRIMS). As of May 2017, the MOI verified that 70 percent of its personnel, which includes the ANP, are enrolled in AHRIMS – an increase of 35 percent within a quarter. The enrolment of both the ANA and the ANP in AHRIMS is scheduled to be completed by end of 2017. The incomplete registration of personnel nevertheless underlines the risk of "ghost" personnel. Therefore, the establishment of AHRIMS in addition to the Afghan Personnel Pay System (APPS) increases transparency and tackles the risk of not-existing staff on public payrolls (SIGAR 2017, 101-103). Yet the longstanding uncertainty about the true number of policemen leaves marks on the overall efficiency and effectiveness of training measures.

4.2.3. Assessing the Reconstruction of the Police

The preceding sections summarised the cornerstones, advancements and limitations of the police advisory mission. In the following, these developments feed into the indicator-based assessment framework (as presented in section 3.2) complemented by further information concerning each evaluation criterion.

The first evaluation criterion concerns the relevance and appropriateness of the police reconstruction efforts. The international coalition had to deal with the significant lack of education, factionalised affiliations and even criminal behaviour of usually self-appointed police officers. The low literacy among the ANP was addressed in a systematic matter only after seven years of international intervention, though it was a root of inadequate logistical, administrative and communicative abilities. While the time factor to establish a functional security system has to be considered, the neglect of lacking basic skills limits the extent to which SSR was suited to the target group. Particularly, illiterate trainees could hardly follow the simply recycled PowerPoint-presentations from previous advisory missions (Giustozzi and Kalinovsky 2016, 262-263).

Yet the changing reform approach indicates some adaptiveness to changing circumstances. Previous concepts were overthrown when proven to be inefficient, e.g. the FDD approach. Nevertheless, many observers point out that the agenda hardly balanced short- and long-term considerations, but focused on "'quick fix' solutions that prioritise the quantity of police over the quality" (Wilder 2007, xi). Furthermore, there was significant friction within the international community concerning the right approach to police reform in Afghanistan, which also affected the coherence of efforts. The dual programmes divided over the paramilitary or civilian role of the police reflect a missing consensus of security threats and needs of the Afghan state and citizens. Consequently, the focus on counterinsurgency impeded sufficient anti-crime and other policing capabilities of the ANP recognised by the U.S. DOD (2017, 76). The overall advisory implementation can thus be assessed at level 4 with unsatisfactory results significantly below expectations. For example, the UNESCO (2016, 25) observed improvements of police literacy, albeit remaining below the target.

Apart from that, the ANP can boast the highest percentage of female personnel in the ANDSF of 2 percent (2,881 women) as of May 2017. Even though this number sounds small, it is above the ANDSF average of 1.3 percent indicating an increasing orientation at women's security needs (SIGAR 2017, 119). Due to Afghanistan's conservative culture concerning the role of women in addition to the above mentioned poor reputation of the ANP, even a low 2-percent women rate represents noteworthy progress for the recruitment and inclusion of women.

The efforts in gender mainstreaming add to the next evaluation criterion: effectiveness. The overall number of policemen increased, best illustrated by the force strength of 148,710 ANP as of April 2017. Yet this number is still below the target end-strength of 1570,000 compounded by high attrition rates (DOD 2017, 76-77). Furthermore, the police still lack sufficient ammunition and vehicles (Katzman and Thomas 2017, 35). Although improvements were made in terms of registration, thus validation of police personnel, there are still nor trustworthy statistics concerning the real number of the police or respective ghost personnel (SIGAR 2017, 101-103). Previous capability assessments reported – despite their qualitative restriction – lacking capabilities among ANP units (SIGAR 2014a, 5). This data is stale now and the current capability level of the ANP remains obscure due to lacking monitoring capacities. However, it was reported that, as of May 2017, 13 percent of the ALP and 2.4 percent of the ANP were untrained. The ALP thus hangs behind the commitment benchmark of no more than 5 percent untrained forces (SIGAR 2017, 104, 117). Concerning the goal of multi-ethnicity, significant progress in balancing the police force was made. In 2002, Tajiks and Uzbeks were strongly overrepresented in the force, whereas the composition has been increasingly rebalanced concerning Pashtun and Hazara inclusion. By 2010, the overall ANP represented a multi-ethnic force, although in some segments (e.g. the officer corps) certain groups such as the Tajiks remain overrepresented (Giustozzi and Isaqzadeh 2013, 106-108). All things considered, the overall effectiveness level is curtailed to a level 3 with satisfactory results yet below the expectations.

Efficiency, on the contrary, lags behind the level of effectiveness of the mission. The need for retraining policemen whose abilities regressed, plus repeatedly discarding training approaches like the FDD as futile, suggests that the chosen steps were not cost-efficient (Giustozzi and Isaqzadeh 2013, 50). The organisational model itself, with the dual programme of Germany/EUPOL and the U.S. on the other side, overlapped in their tasks compromising efficiency (Giustozzi and Kalinovsky 2016, 272-273). However, it was tried to enhance efficiency with the establishment of EUPOL and the NTM-A, though the re-organisation did not fully resolve the inadequacies and frictions remained. Moreover, the advisory mission failed to incorporate research results of the U.S. Government Accountability Office (by name in charge of efficient disbursement) or SIGAR that reiterated deficiencies, e.g. of the capability rating or resource distribution (Sopko 2016, 5). Thus efficiency is rated with level 5 for clearly inadequate results despite some partial positive developments.

Concerning the impact of advisory efforts, the female ratio in the ANP illustrates an improved access for women to the police and education opportunities. Despite this positive development, there are outside assessments that citizens mistrust or even fear the police (Katzman and Thomas 2017, 35). Considering the entry point for reform and the reputation of the police as robbers, the intended improvement in reputation and professionalization advanced but hardly matured (Wilder 2007, xii). The police is reportedly involved in local factional or ethnic disputes. Recurrent claims about human rights abuses of the ALP undermine credibility towards the international reformers and the Afghan government. The emergence of private security forces (e.g. the arbokai) express citizen's feelings of insecurity, but also reflect weak police coverage, not to mention a challenge to the state's monopoly on violence (Katzman and Thomas 2017, 35-37). Moreover, the illegal selling of police equipment affects the police's sustainability and fuels inadvertently criminality or even insurgency (Katzman and Thomas 2017, 35). In brief, the impact of police reform is rated at level 5 as negative impressions currently prevail and efforts to eradicate the deficiencies still need to unfold.

Assessing the sustainability of the force, negative predictions dominated even among the trainers and advisors (Giustozzi and Kalinovsky 2016, 264). The high attrition rate illustrates a major challenge to sustainability which were hitherto compensated by positive recruitment statistics. The loss of trained and experienced officers affects long-term prospects of the police in terms of knowledge sharing, maintenance of material or procedures, and the overall stability of the institution. The MOI is still struggling with police training planning and budgeting (DOD 2017, 71-72). Concerning financial sustainability, the Afghan police is currently highly dependent on international funding. Particularly, as the ALP is completely financed by the United States (SIGAR 2017, 116). At the Warsaw Summit in July 2016, NATO committed to contribute to the sustainment of ANDSF until the end of 2020. The aim is that, by end of 2024, Afghanistan will take full financial responsibility for its forces (NATO 2016). At the NATO Chicago Summit 2012, the Afghan government pledged to contribute $500 million annually for the ANDSF. Although it has not yet reached this goal, the international community accepted Afghanistan's contributions as meeting the obligations due to the serious security situation. After all, Ghani's administration increased the security funds from $387 million in 2016 to a budgeted $400 million in 2017 showing growing commitment and ownership (DOD 2017, 85). Nevertheless, it seems unlikely that the Afghan government will attain financial self-sufficiency for its security forces until the end of 2024. The World Bank estimates that Afghanistan will not meet its public spending needs in the near future, but remains dependent on donor funding even in the best-case scenarios (SIGAR 2017, 58). Acknowledging the recent progress towards sustainability and ownership, this category receives a level 3 rating. Up to now, the ANP and ALP remain highly dependent on international support and the NUG has been unable to contain attrition.[39] Level 3 also signals that although the situation is likely to decline significantly without international support, the overall developmental efficacy remains positive in view of the remodelled training institutions.

International coherence of efforts was significantly compromised by the dual organisations resulting from discarding the lead nation approach. This resulted in a collision of donor priorities that eventually hampered the development of sufficient anti-crime abilities of the ANP. The multinational character of the mission contributed to fragmented policies that clearly lacked cooperation. The European advisory mission did not accept a proposal of CSTC-A to establish a joint reporting to the U.S.-led NTM-A. ISAF itself lacked coherence; interaction between its different elements (ISAF headquarter, NTM-A and CSTC-A) was reportedly flawed. Altogether, the international reformers did not establish a holistic approach (Giustozzi and Kalinovsky 2016, 273-274, 282). Quite the contrary, the police reform efforts were described as being "ad hoc, disaggregated, and poorly defined" (Hughes 2014, 3). With EUPOL's termination by end of 2016 and the smaller RS mission in place, coordination issues have diminished. The RS operation remains of multi-national character, whose impact on coherence has yet to be seen. Prior to this, under EUPOL and ISAF, the reconstruction approach overlooked cross-sectoral dependencies. The justice system, for example, was neglected in terms of advising and funding. Consequently, the inoperative court and prison system subverted the police reform (Hammes 2015, 295). Apart from this, the ANA and the Afghan Ministry of Defence (MOD) received much greater attention, thus funds and advisers, than the MOI and the ANP. As of 30 June 2017, the United States DOD disbursed about $41.94 billion for the ANA and only roughly half of this, $20.8 billion, for the ANP (SIGAR 2017, 71). Though the amount of money spent does not indicate the quality of results, it reveals the imbalanced state-building approach (and U.S. priorities). So far, the ANP lags behind the ANA in its development; on the ministerial level, the MOI lags behind the MOD in its capacities e.g. concerning training (DOD 2017, 71, 76). The performance gap between these pillars of the security system illustrates the disregard of a

39 Remember that sustainability has only a 4-point rating scale (see section 3.2). Level 3 is the second worst rating possible. Level 4 signals that the situation is "very unlikely to improve" or "very likely to deteriorate severely" (KfW 2015, 7). As we have observed some progress in this category instead of an implosion of the police after ISAF's withdrawal, the rating is lifted to a level 3.

"whole-of-government"-mechanisms resulting in a level 5 rating of this category.

Shifting attention to the coordination between multiple components of the security system (reform), it was already noted that the creation of the ALP conflicted and even partially reversed DDR-measures (Katzman and Thomas 2017, 37). Despite that, the MOI struggled with its own patchwork organisation originating from the assignment of posts to different ethnicities after the Bonn Agreement. This resulted in pervasive patronage networks and widespread corruption obstructing the MOI's professionalization (Giustozzi and Kalinovsky 2016, 266). Communication structures were only weakly institutionalised and relied upon personal relations, which inhibited forging strategic cooperation, even between the internationals and the MOI (Giustozzi and Isaqzadeh 2013, 52). Police mentors were typically not briefed about the Afghan legal system before deploying to the country undermining strategic oversight. The lack of mentors in certain departments of the MOI further impeded systematic coordination between different parts of the security system. For example, the anti-corruption unit of the MOI was left without any mentoring until 2010-11 (Giustozzi and Kalinovsky 2016, 275, 281). As corruption is described one of the greatest challenges for the MOI and the ANP, lacking mentoring signifies a strategic gap in the mission. Established in 2009, the Major Crimes Task Force (MCTF) of the MOI and the Anti-Corruption Justice Center, created in November 2016, investigate major corruption cases (SIGAR 2017, 92). Although these institutions illustrate progress towards cross-sectoral reform, they faced considerable resistance. SIGAR (2017, 151) emphasised "the Afghan government still needs to take ownership of and empower the MCTF, which Resolute Support sees as 'swimming against the tide' of the general state of Afghan government corruption." Moreover, cross-pillar communication between the MOI and the MOD remains weak, yet President Ghani initiated a reform to align the ministries to improve coordination and command in early 2017 (DOD 2017, 2, 39). Besides, the women rate in the ANP proves some progress to incorporate gender empowerment programmes in the police system. In view of the current situation and the long-term gaps in coordinating different parts of the security system (especially under ISAF and EUPOL), the overall rating for this category is set at level 4. However, if the recent positive trend in strengthening coordination and communication continues, the rating level will likely rise in the coming years.

The last rating criterion explores the extent to which SSR efforts have promoted key principles and values in security governance (OECD 2011b,

49-50). The advisory mission shows a mixed record in transparency and accountability. While SIGAR or the U.S. GAO regularly published progress reports, these institutions also criticized wasted funds in reform process (Sopko 2016, 5). Furthermore, the mere necessity of the ALP underlines that equal access to regular police, as a principle of security governance, has not been achieved. The effective promotion of good governance, rule of law and respect for human rights turns out deficient regarding the above-described pervasive corruption, accusations of human rights abuses, or involvement in factional or ethnic disputes. UNAMA reports with concern that the government fails to investigate allegations of human rights abuses of governmental forces and to prosecute the perpetrators, in particular concerning the ALP (UNAMA 2017, 96-98). In April 2017, the International Crisis Group summarised the defective structure of the police:

> "The ANP and ALP are, moreover, ridden with corruption and nepotism. ANP officer appointments are often patronage based; staff positions are stacked with junior and inexperienced officers, appointed due to nepotism, corruption or simply the ability to read and write." (International Crisis Group 2017b, 15)

Consequently, the category "consistency with values" receives a level 5 rating as the current condition of the police system is dominated by poor results concerning the promotion of key principles and values in security governance.

Figure 3 summarises the assessment ratings for the international police reform. The overall average is 4.25, hence the results were unsatisfactory and significantly below expectations. The rating also means that the situation has improved in general; no category received the level 6 rating, which would mean a deteriorated situation after the intervention. Yet the overall rating reflects that the reform missed its original targets as presented in section 4.2.1. The force has been increasingly balanced towards multi-ethnicity and the original target of 62,000 policemen was already exceeded more than twice. Given the quality of the results, the police force has proven to lack sustainability, professionalism and a full commitment to the rule of law. The ratings acknowledge that President Ghani and Resolute Support have taken significant steps to further reform the ANDSF, albeit these measures still have to unfold. That being said, detailed insights into the development of the police and the military have been increasingly limited due to the withdrawal of international advisors. Then again, the assessment provides only an aggregated external assessment, whereas the capabilities, performance and leadership of the police are reported to vary from district to district (Hammes 2015, 300).

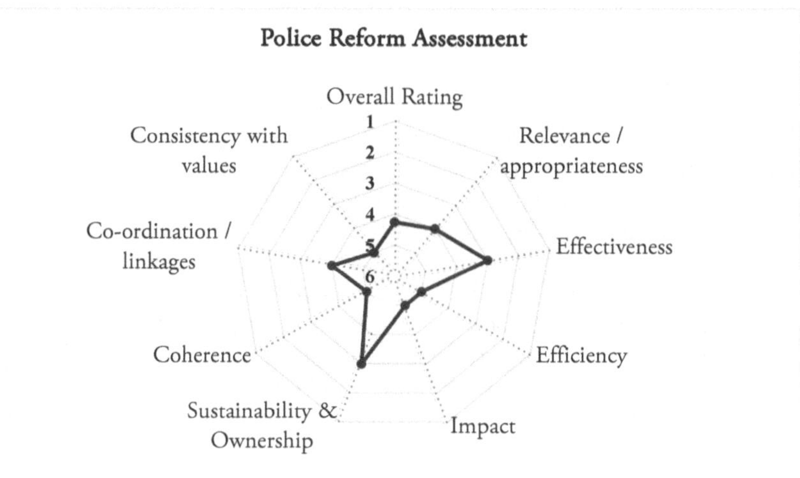

Figure 3: Police Reform Rating (Source: own figure)

4.3. The Afghan Military

The military reconstruction analysis applies the same structure as the police chapter in order to facilitate the comparison of both programmes. Following the assessment of the process under the evaluation framework in section 4.3.3., the study draws together the sectoral findings in view of the overarching SSR and state-building approach (4.4).

4.3.1. The Military Reform Agenda Starting from Scratch

The point of departure for military reconstructions was similar to the one of the police. The military as a formal institution had disintegrated under the Taliban and so did formal training, etc. Again, the whole institution had to be re-build basically from scratch (Katzman and Thomas 2017, 34). At the December 2002 conference in Bonn, it was agreed (again without setting a deadline) that "the new Afghan army should be ethnically balanced, voluntary, and consist of no more than 70,000 individuals (including all civilian and Ministry of Defense personnel)" (U.S. GAO 2005, 6). Further aims of the rebuilding included loyalty to the state government, discipline, professionalization, affordability and sustainability (Giustozzi and Kalinovsky 2016, 239).

As described above, the United States assumed the lead of ANA reconstruction. Before the U.S. Special Forces arrived in Afghanistan in May 2002, ISAF had already started with instructing single battalions called kandak (Hammes 2015, 279). The first wave of U.S. training by the Special Forces was similarly fragmented and conducted the mission without a clearly defined institutional and organisational framework. This changed in October 2002, when the U.S.-led Office of Military Cooperation-Afghanistan (OMC-A) was created (Giustozzi and Kalinovsky 2016, 241). Its first chief, Major General Karl Eikenberry (USA), realized that the mission was of too small-scale and needed to be refocused from a subnational to the national level. He further recognised the lack of basic army infrastructure and equipment including a recruiting force, trainers and living facilities. In 2003, Task Force Phoenix was established as part of the OMC-A tasked to train the Afghan army (Hammes 2015, 279-280). This decision was the first step in creating an organisational structure criticized as "confusing, impenetrable, and top-heavy" (Helmer 2008, 80). Phoenix concentrated on training the lower army levels (the lowest company levels and next higher battalion level), but also began working on the regional brigade and the corps level. However, it fell short of sufficient personnel to cover the national-level institutions like the MOD, which was contracted out to a private U.S. security company called Military Professional Resources, Incorporated (MPRI)[40].

Apart from that, the basic training structure rested on a multinational division of labour. The 4-week basic training course was entrusted to the Afghans supported by U.S. advisers. The French conducted the officers' course and the British the non-commissioned officers' (NCO) training at the Kabul army academy (Hammes 2015, 280). In field, the "Embedded Training Teams" (ETTs) staffed exclusively with U.S. personnel or "Operational Mentoring Liaison Teams" consisting of Non-Americans mentored the Afghan units (Giustozzi and Kalinovsky 2016, 245). This multinational structure assembled diverging military cultures, which compounded effective cooperation when the forces joined their companies and battalions after their graduation from training. In addition, Soviet-trained or former Mujahedeen soldiers brought along additional values and experiences that further compli-

[40] In 2010, MPRI was superseded by DynCorp for mentoring the MOD – a decision of high controversy as the MPRI offer was reportedly 25 percent cheaper (Giustozzi and Kalinovsky 2016, 261-262).

cated unification and collaboration (Hammes 2015, 280-281). The integration of these former fighters posed a challenge to the international mission. For the international community the major concern was to introduce war criminals and factionalism into the army. From an Afghan point of view, however, it was of critical importance to ensure ethnic balance in the ANA. In order to compromise these priorities, a careful vetting and dialogue process that also included political leaders was conducted before assigning applicants to key billets (ibid., 281). Furthermore, tensions were reported between Soviet-trained and former Mujahedeen fighters in the ANA – and even between different factions of the latter. The internal quarrels resulted in disrespectful behaviour and impeded effective mentoring and cooperation within the ANA and beyond in the MOD in Kabul (Giustozzi and Kalinovsky 2016, 268).

By 2005, the international mission announced significant progress in the reconstruction of the Afghan army, but admitted major challenges at the same time. Training for army battalions was formalised and standardised at 14 weeks with six weeks of individual, six weeks of advanced, and two more weeks of collective training.[41] Classes included human rights issues, as well as laws of war. Specialized training in maintenance, logistics or medical support was also conducted (U.S. GAO 2005, 12). By July 2005, the ANA consisted of 24,300 trained and equipped forces and OMC-A expected to meet the target of 46,000 forces by fall of 2007 (Hammes 2015, 283). The overall reconstruction of the army was planned to be completed by fall of 2009 (U.S. GAO 2005, 6). Comparing this quantity to the number of police, the army rebuilding process had a slow start. Until 2005, the dual police advisory missions had trained more than 35,000 forces and planned to achieve their target of 62,000 by the end of the year (ibid., 19-20). In contrast to the police programme, however, the military mission already incorporated ethnic considerations by establishing recruiting stations in each of Afghanistan's 34 provinces to ensure that volunteers of all ethnicities had a chance of joining the army (ibid., 11).[42]

The GAO 2005-report notes key challenges to army reform that were repeatedly described at later stages of the process and reveal some similarities

41 As pointed out in section 4.2.1 a similar multi-stage process was not applied to the police, but consisted out of an eight weeks basic training course for fresh recruits and only two weeks training for veteran police (in addition to the shortened four-week programme for illiterate officers).

42 The establishment of recruitment stations did not automatically lead to an ethnically balanced force, as we will show below.

to those of the police reform. First, the numerous changes in plan and personnel complicated the mission. Second, the ANA experienced shortages of critical equipment. Third, there were significant challenges concerning the quality and composition of recruits plus ethnic disputes (ibid., 14-15, 19).

Taking a closer look at each of these problems, the change in plans and personnel already occurred in the pre-2005 advisory efforts. Turnover in organisation, staff and targets affected the mission several times until today. Starting with the OMC-A, it was renamed to Office of Security Cooperation-Afghanistan (OSC-A) in 2005, when it assumed responsibility for the U.S. efforts to raise the ANP (Hammes 2015, 283, 293). In April 2006, OSC-A was replaced by the CSTC-A. Task Force Phoenix remained in place as the command's direct sub-ordinate facilitator (Giustozzi and Kalinovsky 2016, 241). In June 2009, CSTC-A became part of ISAF within the NTM-A, as described in section 4.2.1 (Hammes 2015, 285). With the completion of NTM-A, CSTC-A shifted under the Resolute Support mission as the U.S. budget executing organisation without being directly involved in training and advising (ibid., 291). Furthermore, the ETTs and OMLTs were denominated in 2012, when new mentoring plans for transition were approved. The U.S. staffed ETTs became Security Force Assistance Advisory Teams (SFAATs) and the non-American staffed OMLTs were turned into Military Assistance Teams (MATs) (Giustozzi and Kalinovsky 2016, 245-246). Although this description is quite a brief history of the mission's re-organisation, it illustrates the challenge of tracking the reconstruction process with regards to changing designations and tasks. The organisational structure evolved so complicated that U.S. Captain Daniel Helmer noted: "The structure is so confusing that it is almost painful to describe" (Helmer 2008, 80). He further experienced that authority structures were so opaque that it was often unclear who was in charge that day and work was regularly passed in cycles waiting for more agreeable tasks or avoiding decisions (ibid.).[43]

In addition to these organisational changes, targets for the ANA reconstruction were altered several times. Similar to the police reform process, the target numbers might differ significantly in documents because the composition of the target size (e.g. with or without ministry or civilian personnel) varies without explanation. For the ANA, there were at least four major increases in target sizes during the reform process, apart from several smaller ones. In 2008 alone, there were two major increases in size goals for the ANA: In early 2008, the target force size was revised up to 80,000 and by fall of the same year to 134,000 ANA forces. At the January 2010 London conference,

[43] This also refers to the U.S. police advisory mission which was considered in its rating e.g. for coherence and efficiency.

target end-strengths were adjusted upwards to 171,000 (U.S. GAO 2011, 3-4). In August 2011, the goal was raised again, now aiming for 195,000 ANA forces to be reached by November 2012 – for the time being, this was the last adjustment of targets (Hammes 2015, 289).[44]

The steady increase in target size is related to growing security threats reflected by an upward trend of attacks recognised by the international community. However, each revision was made before the original target was achieved (U.S. GAO 2011, 3-4). This reveals the problematic nature of steady changes in plans and growing target requirements. Even in 2005, when targets were modest compared to 2011, the OMC-A lacked sufficient personnel. According to the GAO, up to 2005, "OMC-A has never been staffed at more than about 71 percent of its approved personnel level" (U.S. GAO 2005, 15). Manning gaps remained and even worsened as by 2010, NTM-A was staffed at 52 percent of its authorized personnel (Hammes 2015, 286). In the field, the personnel gap resulted in lacking monitoring units hampering the goal to cover the whole ANA. The gap persisted until transition started in 2011 and staffing requirements went down (Giustozzi and Kalinovsky 2016, 252-253).

Growing targets also affected the second challenge stated above: the lack of equipment for the ANA. Already in 2005, the GAO reported equipment shortages for uniforms, boots, weapons, ammunition, vehicles, and other basic army supplies. OMC-A tried to mitigate the problem, but as it neglected quality control, ordered items turned out faulty (U.S. GAO 2005, 14-15). As reported by GAO (2005, 16): "U.S. trainers told us that Afghan troops sometimes wore sandals during operations in mountainous, difficult terrain because their boots had failed." In the following years, shortages of critical equipment remained. By 2008, the GAO noted a gap of 40 percent of critical ANA equipment (Hammes 2015, 285). Three years later, still various shortages persisted, even though the GAO acknowledged some improvements (U.S. GAO 2011, 23). Recent reports do not include detailed information on the overall equipment level anymore. In its July 2017-report SIGAR only described a lack in operational readiness for the equipment, which was on average around 68 percent. On the one hand, there was an overall increase in operational readiness across all ANA combat elements (SIGAR 2017, 108). On the other hand, the U.S. DOD warns that inconsistent and inaccurate reporting of operational readiness impedes the estimation of equipment levels and capabilities (DOD 2017, 45). As a consequence

44 Similarly, target force sizes were revised upwards for the police (Hammes 2015, 284-289).

of poor equipment, ANA effectiveness, but also discipline was hampered according to trainers in the field (U.S. GAO 2005, 14). Fighting next to best equipped forces like U.S. soldiers, the Afghans felt being used as "cannon fodder" (Giustozzi and Isaqzadeh 2013, 52).[45]

Problems concerning equipment are also related to the third challenge mentioned above, the quality and composition of recruits. Comparable to the ANP, the majority of army recruits was illiterate. Giustozzi and Kalinovsky (2016, 262) present sources that for a while evidence stated that 90 percent of the army recruits were illiterate and the rest was hardly educated beyond primary school. The problems connected to poor literacy as well as the process of recognition and solution by the NTM-A was the same for the army as for the police described in section 4.2.1. Yet, the results of literacy courses have not been estimated by the UNESCO (2016) study cited above. As Katzman and Thomas (2017, 33) point out, it is unlikely that the goals of an overall first-grade literacy and at least 50 percent third grade literacy have been achieved. The issue is of two-fold meaning to the ANA: The foreign advisors did not only struggle with teaching the recruits with traditional methods, but also lacked qualified leaders for the army to rebuild. In early 2008, as much as 50 percent of all ANA non-commissioned officer positions were unfilled. The situation improved by 2011, when a quarter (8,413) of all NCO positions was vacant (U.S. GAO 2011, 23). By 2012, the number of needed ANA NCO increased again to 10,600 (U.S. GAO 2012, 6).[46] Apart from missing skills in the army to fill these vacancies, the GAO accounted the lack of advisers and the growing requirements in size for missing leader candidates – illustrating the interconnectedness of the challenges presented (U.S. GAO 2012, 24; 2011, 6). Even in 2017, leadership remains an issue for the army and for the Afghan security system as a whole (DOD 2017, 38). In addition, lacking specialized skills ranging from maintenance and logistical skills to English-speaking candidates still present points of concern to the ANA (ibid., 61-62).

Despite all efforts for ethnic balancing, the ANA experienced significant difficulties recruiting sufficient numbers of southern Pashtuns. These people were reluctant joining the ANA as an instrument of the central government, which was formed by the Northern Alliance. They perceived the Northern Alliance as an occupying force as it was dominated by Uzbeck and Hazara to whom traditional animosities exist (Hammes 2015, 289). In order to create

45 As noted before, this concerns similar to the police that even traditionally suffered higher casualty rates than the ANA (SIGAR 2017, 106).

46 For the ANP a similar gap was observable with around 8,300 unfilled NCOs (U.S. GAO 2012, 6).

greater ethnic balance, quotas have been introduced for the ANA which led to an increase of Pashtun recruits from 2004 onwards. For a long time, the MOD denied balancing issues, but statistics proved that Tajiks were overrepresented in the army (Giustozzi 2015, 139-140).

Ethnicity is reported to affect both the internal relations in the army and the external relations between the ANA and society. Regarding the first, the communication and cooperation between officers of different ethnicities was hampered as sometimes witnessed that they refused to talk to each other (Giustozzi and Kalinovsky 2016, 266). Concerning the second issue, the ANA struggled to establish constructive relations to local authorities or populations, especially in the (Pashtun dominated) south when Tajik commanders tried to establish the contact (Giustozzi 2015, 138). Even though the quota system was reported ineffective, there were also concerns raised that an ethnic quota for all levels of the ANA would compromise meritocratic selection of candidates (ibid., 140). This in turn may be related to the abovementioned lack of qualified leaders. In sum, the overall composition of the army, lacking education in the force, missing key skills and equipment, and constant changes of plan turn out to be interrelated challenges whose impact on the overall capabilities of the ANA and transition to Afghan security responsibility needs to be observed in the following sections.

4.3.2. The Military under Transition to Full Responsibility

In 2009, even before the termination of ISAF was announced, a new approach to ANA advising was introduced: the embedded partnering approach. The reformed approach required ANA units taking over responsibilities with ISAF teams mentoring them on a one-to-one-basis – not to be confused to person-to-person mentoring (Giustozzi and Kalinovsky 2016, 281). In the run-up to training and mentoring reforms in 2009, capability assessments of the ANA found significant shortfalls in performance despite some major advances. In April 2008, only two ANA units (less than 2 percent of the 105 units rated) were assessed fully capable of conducting primary missions; eight months later, in December 2008, the DOD reported 18 (around 25 percent of the 72 units rated) fully capable (U.S. GAO 2009, 19). The quality of this rating was questioned and completely revised in September 2010, when ISAF found that none of the 163 ANA units rated was capable of conducting its mission independently (U.S. GAO 2011, 21). These diverging estimations of capabilities, as well as different numbers of units included, reflect the questionable quality of the rating system as explained in section 4.2.2.

Apart from rating results, the need of ANA units to run additional two to four weeks of training confirmed inadequate capabilities and unsuccessful basic courses. Soldiers were found to graduate from training without being able to carry out basic duties or to shoot straight. Advisers reported many absent recruits missing third to half of the classes – reportedly, they were pressured to let them pass anyway (Giustozzi and Kalinovsky 2016, 290). In view of these shortcomings, General Caldwell reformed basic training in 2009. Yet, even after reform, Giustozzi and Kanilovsky (2016, 290) regard the advisory concept too much focused on quick wins as for example firing tests required the recruits to shot two magazines without grading their ability to aim.

With the partnering approach, more than just formal procedures were innovated. The new ISAF commander General Stanley McChrystal (USA) identified a considerable alienation between the internationals, the ANA forces and the Afghan population as a central failure of SSR (Hammes 2015, 286). Up to 2010, the international forces would lead their lives in the country separated from their Afghan mentees. Interaction between foreign advisers and Afghans was very limited, even during their joint patrols (Giustozzi and Kalinovsky 2016, 326). By contrast, the U.S.-American counterinsurgency field manual 3-24, released in 2006, dictated that segregation ought to be kept "at an absolute minimum" and advisers are expected to "live, work, and (when authorized) fight with their HN units" (U.S. Army and U.S. Marince Corps 2006, 6-17). McChrystal recognised the manuals lacking implementation in Afghanistan and ordered the creation of shared dining establishments and sleeping quarters. This was, however, not appreciated by all international advisers (Giustozzi and Kalinovsky 2016, 326).

The relation between Afghans and their advisers was pervaded with mutual distrust. Among internationals, negative views about their mentees prevailed. Advisers complained about the low level of education and reported that ANA soldiers showed little will to fight, even hided or fled from enemy forces leaving behind equipment and vehicles to be captured by Taliban (Giustozzi 2015, 174, 180). British Army officer Graham Lee gives an insight into the negative perceptions of the foreigners: "According to some in the British Army, the Afghan Army was incompetent, lazy, cowardly, backward and gay" (Lee 2012, 136).

Similarly, there are reports that the Afghans felt disrespected or even abused by their foreign counterparts. Complaints were raised about missing language skills, arrogant and rough behaviour, disrespect for cultural values and disregard of the local mentality (Krüger 2014, 90). Foreign forces joking about their peers was understood by the Afghans without translation and created resentment. Senior soldiers assigned to basic courses led by young advisers considered this treatment as discourteous (Giustozzi and Kalinovsky

2016, 263, 316-318). Additionally, insider attacks[47] increasingly occurred since 2007 and further poisoned the relations between Afghans and coalition forces (Krüger 2014, 90, U.S. GAO 2013, 18). Introducing the partnering approach aimed therefore to transform the relations between Afghans and international staff by applying a different language, i.e. becoming equal partners. In contrast to this, the Afghans sensed an imbalanced relation inherent in the concepts of advising and mentoring. Calling them partners was hence interpreted an approach "to appease Afghan sensitivities" (Giustozzi and Kalinovsky 2016, 318).

In practice, international staff continued wearing body armour for example during meetings – an indication of distrust and disrespect from an Afghan perspective but justified due to threatening security situation in the foreigners' view (ibid., 326). Despite vetting measures for fresh recruits and precautions like vehicle searches, insider attacks could not be prevented, but even became more frequent. In 2012, the number of foreign forces killed by insider attacks reached a peak: over 60 were killed, in contrast to 33 in 2011, and 16 in 2010 (ibid., 325). Reports assessed these attacks a systematic hazard to the lives of the deployed forces; NATO reacted by ordering all allied forces to wear loaded firearms and reducing joint missions with the ANA (Krüger 2014, 88). Although the number of green-on-blue attacks was successfully reduced, the total number of insider attacks, particularly green-on-green, has been on the rise again. The number of attacks has surpassed the 2012-level of 46 attacks with 62 reported insider attacks in 2015 (57 green-on-green, five green-on-blue) and 60 in 2016 (56 green-on-green, four green-on-blue) according to SIGAR (2017, 90). Its continued relevance was described in the introduction of the thesis referring to the attacks in Kabul and Masar-i-Sharif (Webermann 2017). SIGAR calls this incident "the most serious potential insider attack that occurred this quarter" (SIGAR 2017, 90). The recurring incidents do not only testify lacking capabilities of the ANA – and of the international community – to eradicate endogenous threats, but also exacerbated the climate of suspicion (Giustozzi and Kalinovsky 2016, 325). As a result, Krüger (2014, 90) declared the concept of partnering has failed, albeit nobody wants to officially admit it.

Comparable to the police reconstruction mission, capability assessments gained importance in the run-up to ISAF's termination. Security threats by insider attacks and the poor rating of September 2010, when not a single ANA unit was assessed fully capable to conduct its mission, underline the

[47] Insider attacks are categorized into "green-on-blue" attacks when Afghan forces turn on coalition personnel, or "green-on-green" when Afghans are attacked by forces from their own ranks (SIGAR 2017, 90).

hardships in rebuilding the army (U.S. GAO 2011, 21). The high dependency on coalition assistance was stressed, especially coupled with the ANA's lacking capabilities. Giustozzi and Kalinovsky (2016) emphasise the development of a syndrome of dependency among Afghan units as "probably the worst heritage of the massive advisory mission" (294). The problem does not only refer to the still persistent donor dependency of the Afghan government to sustain its force, but to reliance on international assistance in the daily tasks of the army (DOD 2017, 85). Advisers noted for example lacking logistical skills and high dependency on coalition air support. The roots of these problems are commonly traced back to the above described low levels of education in the ANA in addition to coalition fallacies. A problem-solving attitude was observed among mentors, finding expression in taking over command or organisational tasks and showing little patience for their peers to develop their own solutions (Giustozzi and Kalinovsky 2016, 294, 298). As a consequence, in 2009, ISAF issued a directive to influence not direct the Afghan forces (ibid., 299). The 2013 ISAF Security Force Assistance Guide orders advisers to force the Afghans to operate independently and iterates that ISAF must neither command nor lead Afghan units. Instead it should train Afghan forces as well as provide advice and resources if needed (NATO 2013, 11, 21).

Yet the political will to eradicate the ANA's dependency slowly prevailed in 2011 to 2012 – leaving little time to achieve it until ISAF's completion (Giustozzi and Kalinovsky 2016, 294, 297). As Figure 4 illustrates, only 20 out of 204 ANA units were assessed independent with advisers[48], less than 10 percent of the whole army (SIGAR 2014a, 5). In view of the upcoming transition, the international coalition revised its mentoring approach which led to the above mentioned remodelling of OMLTs to MATs and ETTs to SFAATs in 2012. Their task was to facilitate the transition in the country by gradually lifting off international support (Hammes 2015, 289). First these units were deployed on the kandak level, then they lifted off support to the next highest stage, the brigade level, and finally, by late 2013, to the corps level. Moreover, stricter rules were applied to the formation of these units in order to provide adequate staffing and specialisations in addition to pre-deployment training. Furthermore, advisers at the Kabul Military Training Center were now ordered to only interfere in the lessons in exceptional cases,

48 As in section 4.2.2 explained, the rating system changed its highest level from "independent" to "independent with advisers" in 2011 (U.S. GAO 2012, 3-4). Moreover, the criticism issued concerning the quality and integrity of capability assessments applies equally to the ratings presented for the ANA.

e.g. if recruits were endangered, thus promoting greater ownership and independence (Giustozzi and Kalinovsky 2016, 246). Yet in reality, the mentoring units were still formed late, sometimes only in the country, and often missed a proper combination of rank and skills (Hammes 2015, 289). Besides, the adherence to the transition plan resulted in lacking mentoring for lower units. According to ISAF, there were at least four of the then eight corps were brigades still required assistance (Giustozzi and Kalinovsky 2016, 246).

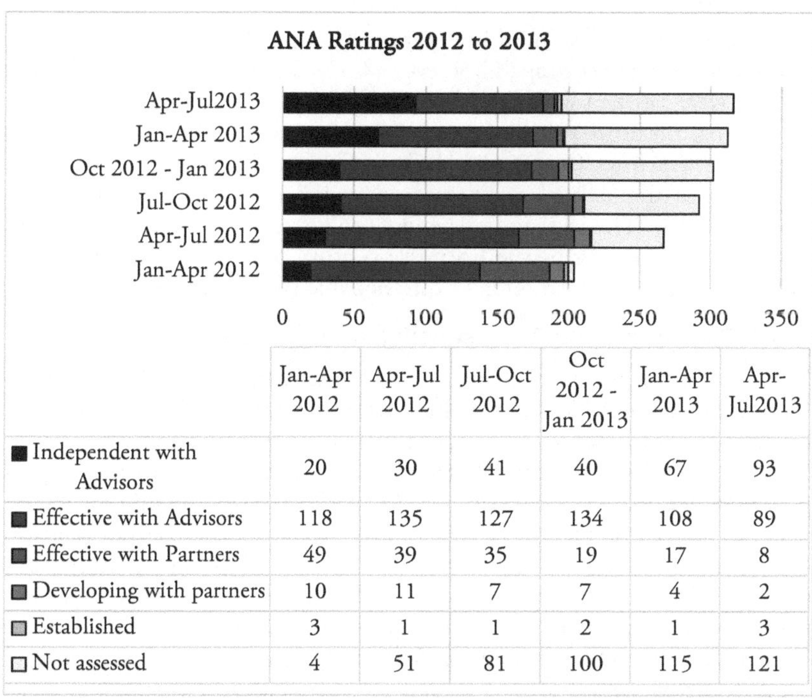

	Jan-Apr 2012	Apr-Jul 2012	Jul-Oct 2012	Oct 2012 - Jan 2013	Jan-Apr 2013	Apr-Jul2013
■ Independent with Advisors	20	30	41	40	67	93
■ Effective with Advisors	118	135	127	134	108	89
■ Effective with Partners	49	39	35	19	17	8
■ Developing with partners	10	11	7	7	4	2
■ Established	3	1	1	2	1	3
□ Not assessed	4	51	81	100	115	121

Figure 4: ANA Ratings 2012-2013 (Source: own figure, data provided by SIGAR 2014a, 5)

Nevertheless, SIGAR noted a step-by-step increase in the capabilities of ANA units. By mid-2013, 93 ANA units received the highest "independent with advisors"-rating, making up almost 30 percent of the force (SIGAR 2014a, 5). However, figure 4 illustrates that similar to the police assessments, the overall monitoring level has significantly decreased since the 2012. In the first assessment period of 2012, almost 98 percent of the ANA units have been assessed (and 93 percent of the ANP units). The latest available rating includes only 62 percent of the ANA units. While this demonstrates waning monitoring capacities and quality, the ANA was still better covered than the ANP of which only 22 percent of its units were assessed in the mid-2013 cycle (ibid., 9). Taking a closer look at the positive trend in the rating, there was, nonetheless, a significant capability gap in mid-2013 and little time left to raise the lower rated units to a level of self-reliance. Its delayed independence is demonstrated by the fact that the first autonomous ANA brigade size operation was only launched in the summer of 2013 (Giustozzi and Kalinovsky 2016, 294).

Due to the withdrawal of international troops, there is little insight left into the army's current capability level. While the Afghan government and NATO were satisfied with the ANA's performance in 2016, there are indications that the army struggles to organise operations and coordinate across command structures (International Crisis Group 2017b, 14-15). As stated above, it was originally planned to complete the army by fall of 2009 (U.S. GAO 2005, 6). The lacking independence illustrated in figure 4, as well as the continued support by the RS mission prove that this target was missed and the ANA's autonomy remains questionable (Giustozzi 2015, 234).

4.3.3. Assessing the Reconstruction of the Military

The information presented above is now fed into the evaluation grid as developed in section 3.2 and complemented by further points of interest about the ANA's reconstruction process, challenges and successes.

The first rating category takes a closer look at the army reform's appropriateness and relevance of measures. The beginnings of the military reconstruction process were, similar to the police reform, characterized as an ad hoc organisation omitting long-term plans to establish sustaining institutions (Hammes 2015, 280, U.S. GAO 2005, 17-18). These challenges were compounded by postponing the management of structural weaknesses in the force such as high illiteracy rates. In August 2010, only around 14 percent of the ANA personnel were found literate at a first grade level – reflecting a gap in professionalization as well as lacking skills to fulfil basic tasks such as recording equipment (U.S. GAO 2011, 24). As described in section 4.2.1, the issue remained of second order until NTM-A took over the reconstruction of both the police and military. However, the established obligatory literacy training remains poorly monitored and executed as SIGAR (2014) revealed. Poor attendance rates to these "mandatory" courses of 50 percent since February 2011, in addition the ANA's high attrition rate of estimated 30 to 50 percent annually, question the long-term success of literacy training (SIGAR

2014b, 10-11). The example illustrates that long- and short-term considerations were hardly balanced with an emphasis on quick wins in quantity for the expense of quality and sustainability (Giustozzi and Kalinovsky 2016, 290).

The reconstruction mission further exhibited technical as well as staffing inadequacies. As shown above, GAO (2011, 25) noted a persistent shortfall in instructors needed for ANA training and mentoring which was not resolved until the gradual lift-off of support. Many instructors lacked language and cultural skills or were too young to be respected by senior personnel (Giustozzi and Kalinovsky 2016, 317). On the plus side of the mission's appropriateness, ethnic tensions, which were at the heart of citizen's security interests, were incorporated into the reconstruction process. The implementation of ethnic balance, however, proved difficult. The current composition of the ANA is indeed multi-ethnic, but not fully balanced (Giustozzi 2015, 139-140).

Concerning the technical adequacy of the mission, logistical shortcomings, the ANA's military doctrine, and inappropriate procurements exemplify the unsuitability of key solutions to the Afghan context. First, the logistical system is already reported a weakness of the ANA by GAO in 2005 in relation to low levels of education (U.S. GAO 2005, 17-18). Even in 2017, logistics remain a central weakness of the Afghan forces (DOD 2017, 37). Giustozzi and Kalinovsky (2016, 297) trace back the roots of the problem to an inappropriate logistical model introduced by the international advisory mission. In 2007, so-called pull logistics have been introduced following the system of the U.S. army. The model is based on bottom-up requests of unit specific needs, in contrast to push logistics that apply a top-down and time-based resupply system. Pull logistics are thus more efficient as they only deliver the supply needed, but they also require a higher amount of coordination and integration. The Afghan forces, however, lacked the literacy level and command coordination needed to apply pull logistics, explaining the traditional push system used by the ANA. As a result, the "Americanized" logistical model evolved into a "largely ineffective hybrid" in which the communication of supply needs and delivery takes several weeks, while some items were still managed by push mechanisms (ibdi.). Similarly, the ANA's military doctrine is repeatedly been criticized to be a "word-for-word translated U.S. doctrine" (Helmer 2008, 80) that is hardly suitable for the Afghan context. By March 2017, a revision to the ANA training doctrine has been announced whose outcome is yet to be seen (DOD 2017, 44).

The third issue raised concerning inappropriate SSR activities were faulty procurements. Apart from the aforementioned mispurchase of boots for the army[49], inappropriate procurements were reported resulting from missing skills in the ANA coupled with a misjudgement of international advisers. The purchase of 20 G222 cargo planes provides a striking example of the inadequate and inefficient decisions made during the advisory mission:

> "SIGAR also has found significant instances of waste and squandered opportunities in the critical area building up the Afghan Air Force. One of the most egregious was DOD's $486 million purchase of 20 G222 medium-lift cargo planes for the Afghan Air Force. Due to poor planning, poor oversight, poor contract management (including possible fraud), and a misunderstanding of aircraft capabilities, those aircraft could not even meet operational requirements in the Afghan setting. The program was ended in March 2013 after experiencing continuous and severe operational difficulties, including a lack of spare parts. Sixteen of those 20 aircraft were sold for scrap metal for six cents a pound or $32,000 in 2013." (Sopko 2016, 14)

According to Hammes (2015), the complexity of these aircrafts "was simply more than the Afghans could manage" (331-332). Currently, significant progress in the development of the Afghan air force is reported, albeit they still lack sufficient specialized personnel (DOD 2017, 54-55).

Since its launch, the mission clearly adapted to the deteriorating security situation reflected by raised target sizes and several re-organisations as described above. All things considered, the reconstruction of the ANA shows unsatisfactory results for relevance and appropriateness, hence a level 4 rating. Although negative results hint for a level 5 rating, the progress being made in the overall development (e.g. regarding ethnic balance) and adjustment of the international efforts lift the rating to a level 4.

Secondly, the effectiveness of the advisory mission has to be assessed. The original target to complete the ANA's reconstruction by 2009 was missed in both quantitative and qualitative regards as shown in the previous sections. As of May 2017, the ANA has still not met its approved target size of 195,000, but was staffed at approximately 174,274 personnel – almost 11 percent below the authorized end-strength.[50] Among them were 1,044 women making up around 0.6 percent of the force (DOD 2017, 51). This is below the average of 1.3 percent in the ANDSF illustrating that the MOD

[49] See section 4.3.1 reported by GAO (2005, 16).

[50] Number without counting civilian personnel (DOD 2017, 51). For May 2017, SIGAR (2017, 100) reports a force strength of around 180,000 ANA personnel including the air force (without civilians), which would still be under the authorized end-strength of 195,000.

is struggling more with gender issues than the MOI (SIGAR 2017, 99, 119). Nonetheless, this number is still a progress considering the Afghan environment in which families disallow their daughters to join the army because of traditional women's roles or concerns for security. However, the ANA continues to struggle with the establishment of adequate women facilities which includes providing a safe environment for female officers (Cordesman and Lin 2015, 116-117).

A major reason for missing the aims in quality and quantity is the ANA's high attrition rate – similar to the ANP as discussed earlier. In fact, this problem is even worse for the military than for the police. The average attrition rate was 2.3 percent for the whole ANA in the first quarter of 2017, but due to high recruitment rates, there was even a small net gain in the army's growth (DOD 2017, 52, SIGAR 2017, 106). The U.S. DOD relates this phenomenon to limited tours of duty and the widespread deployment of the army forces throughout the country, while police officers usually serve in the place they live in. In contrast to ANP personnel, it is prohibited for ANA soldiers to serve in their home areas in order to decrease the risk of political factionalism or influencing (SIGAR 2017, 106). This relates to the point that in summer times or during the harvest, the number of unexcused absences has been observed to go up to 40 percent over the last years (Krüger 2014, 86). Furthermore, many ANA personnel went home to remit their earnings to their families. This cause has lately been eased by the introduction of the electronic payment system (Katzman and Thomas 2017, 34). The enrolment into AHRIMS also serves the purpose of validating and accounting for ANA staff, which has been better implemented by the MOD than by the MOI. As of May 2017, the MOD properly enrolled and accounted for roughly 88 percent of its (including ANA) personnel in AHRIMS, while the MOI only reported around 70 percent enrolled (SIGAR 2017, 102-103). Yet, there are still significant uncertainties about the actual strengths and thus ghost soldiers in certain corps, especially in the 215th Corps in Helmand. Already in the past this corps was a centre of worries as it served in an area of high insurgency and was reportedly plagued by corruption and opacity (ibid., 103). Reports from November 2015 to January 2016 claimed that the 215th Corps was less than 50 percent staffed (Giustozzi and Ali 2016, 3). Until the end of the enrolment process, uncertainty about the true manning levels in the corps remains leaving questions of the overall effectiveness of the ANA's reconstruction as well as sustainability issues.

Despite all concerns raised about the effectiveness of the international mission, it is stressed that the efforts worked out much better for the ANA than for the ANP (Giustozzi and Kalinovsky 2016, 292). Hammes (2015) praises the ANA as an "aggressive, effective fighting force" (291). In 2016, the military was able to repel insurgent advances for example in Kunduz, but it also suffered high casualties and kept being challenged by Taliban offensives and insider attacks. In contrast to the ANP whose performance is poorly rated, the Afghan government and the NATO showed themselves generally satisfied with the ANA (International Crisis Group 2017b, 14-15). Nevertheless, there are still weaknesses in key areas of the army that showed signs of quick decay after the withdrawal of advisors, especially in logistics and planning, but also concerning its general morale (Giustozzi and Ali 2016, 1, 5). Considering all points, the overall effectiveness is rated satisfactory (level 3) as currently positive results stand out of the (nonetheless significant) shortcomings of the process.

Regarding the efficiency of the mission, there are several incidents of wasted funds such as the aforementioned G222 cargo plane purchase or low quality boots (Sopko 2016, 14, U.S. GAO 2015, 15). In June 2017 report, SIGAR describes the U.S. DOD decision of 2007 to buy uniforms for the ANA with a special pattern on it based on the combat uniforms of the U.S. Army. The decision has led to a purchase of more than 1.3 million uniforms through January 2017. These garments were around 40-43 percent more expensive than those of the ANP using a non-proprietary pattern on their uniform. However, there is no evidence that the costly camouflage pattern is more effective, hence, SIGAR recommends to revise the decision for future procurement (SIGAR 2017, 37-38). The uncovering of those incidents by the U.S. GAO or SIGAR demonstrates that measures were in place to ensure transparency and accountability, but they evidently failed to ensure efficiency before a decision was taken.

In view of the organisational structure, the mission has been described as inefficient with regards to complexity and overlapping tasks that undermined supervision and command-structures (Giustozzi and Kalinovsky 2016, 272-273). The convoluted structure hampered timely decisions of the army and police advisory mission as the NTM-A in cooperation with the CSTC-A executed both agendas. In order to enhance efficiency, Helmer (2008, 80) urged the streamlining of command and simplification of structures which required, among others, the dissolution of Task Force Phoenix – in Helmer's view a redundant, thus unnecessary sub-unit. Another puzzle holds the separation of OMLTs/ MATs and ETTs/SFAATs whose distinction remains unclear according to Giustozzi and Kalinovsky (2016, 245). Concerning the efficiency of outcomes, the effectiveness of literacy training and the questionable attendance of recruits have been highlighted by SIGAR (2014, 9, 11) as risking wasted funds. In particular, the neglect of quality in favour of quantity resulted in limited army capabilities and the need for retraining (Hammes 2015, 287). As in the case of the ANP, the risk of repeated cycles of training could have been mitigated with in-depth tuition – albeit this would have resulted in a slower process thus smaller graduation numbers. In view of the constantly raised target sizes, there was inevitably political pressure on the instructors to generate high graduation rates (Giustozzi and Kalinovsky 2016, 290).

Most recently, the implementation of AHRIMS in Afghanistan and the decision to withhold salaries for unaccounted personnel reduces wasted funds and enhances transparency and accountability in the force. The fact that pay-processes are still paper-based in 2017 and the actual force strengths of the ANA remains questionable, curtailed efficient army management in the past (DOD 2017, 43). The failure to introduce electronic systems earlier underlines whole-of-government deficiencies, as it requires literate and technically adept people to feed and maintain the system. Additionally, officials resisted the implementation of such a transparent system as they used fraud to function in their organisations or to enrich themselves – calling for anti-corruption and leadership reforms (Hammes 2015, 297-298).

To sum up this category, even though, the international efforts did not struggle with a similar dual organisation as in the case of the ANP, the overall efficiency is rated clearly inadequate. This level 5 rating derives particularly from the repeatedly reported inefficiently used funds and low quality of outputs that resulted from improper planning and execution.

Concerning the impact of the advisory mission, the statement of Katzman and Thomas (2017) stands out that the "ANA is reportedly highly regarded by Afghans as a symbol of nationhood and factional nonalignment" (34). This positive statement contrasts the ANP's original reputation as "robbers" (Wilder 2007, 2). On the contrary, the ANA lacks political support in the villages and rivalling factions in the ANA and MOD have caused internal struggles weakening the institutions' public image and functionality (Giustozzi and Ali 2016, 11, 13). On the plus, the progress made in recruiting female forces – albeit being below the ANDSF's average – reflects an improvement in women's rights in the society. Even though this advancement should not be overstated in view of persistent challenges, further measures are on their way. In early 2017, the MOD initiated the Gender Occupational Opportunity Development (GOOD) training programme. The GOOD initiative aims to enhance the capabilities of more than 600 women to perform in the ANA, including computer and English learning courses. In addition, the MOD offers the opportunity of higher education to female personnel such as a Bachelor's degree programme at the Dunya University in Kabul (DOD 2017, 50).

With regard to the impact of the ANA on the well-being of the Afghan people in general, it has to be noted that the army had the highest civilian casualty rates among pro-government parties in 2016. UNAMA attributed more than 50 percent of civilian casualties by pro-government forces to the ANA (899 out of 1,733) – in contrast to 135 civilian casualties (around 8 percent) attributed to the ANP (UNAMA 2017, 6 n.20).[51] Weighing up all arguments, the mission had a satisfactory impact (level 3) as positive trends and statements dominate the shortcomings that keep the rating from obtaining higher marks.

The category sustainability and ownership evaluates the continuation of benefits after the withdrawal of donor support and the integration of local people and structures into the reform. Thus, the category overlaps, e.g. with the appropriateness of measures in relation to local traditions, norms and conditions. Incidences like the G222 cargo plane selling or the ANA's copy-paste military doctrine already revealed shortcomings to the ownership of the process. Just as in the case of the police, some equipment and fuel issued to Afghan forces disappeared and was found on sale on local markets – hampering the army's effectiveness and subverting the sustainability of sponsored goods (Giustozzi and Kalinovsky 2016, 265). Still in 2017, the CSTC-A found pilferage and lacking accountability in the corps, albeit noting some progress (SIGAR 2017, 134).

Furthermore, high attrition rates and the resulting need to recruit and train new forces create the same limitations on sustainability and institutional learning for the ANA as for the ANP. As this rate is higher for the ANA, the consequences are correspondingly more serious (DOD 2017, 34-35). Prior attempts to increase retention through pay incentives have failed in the past, so that the international coalition refrained from this idea (SIGAR 2017, 106). The causes of high force attrition are well-known, e.g. poor leadership, poor medical and welfare services for the ANA, poor payment practices, their deployment far away from home and chiefs denying leave, or the demoralising impact of withdrawn international support (Giustozzi 2015, 161-162). Some of these problems are under reform for instance by introducing the electronic pay system APPS or President Ghani's leadership reform. The latter is part of his four year ANDSF Road Map initiated in early 2017 and

51 UNAMA attributed 24 percent of the 11,418 civilian casualties in 2016 to pro-government forces, 61 percent to anti-government forces (mainly the Taliban), 10 percent to ground engagement between the two without being able to identify a specific party (UNAMA 2017, 3, 6).

resulted in the replacement of three ANA corps and several brigade commanders in the first quarter of the year. The MOI is also included in the leadership overhaul that aims at correcting corruption and nepotism by merit-based appointment procedures (SIGAR 2017, 95-96, 101-102).

Concerning the morale of the force, the occurrence of a dependency syndrome was previously described. Dependency had a physical and a psychological component in Afghanistan. Foreign forces delivered equipment, funding and advice, served as a morale booster[52], and even alleviated corruption. When the internationals were withdrawn, the morale and performance of the ANA observably decayed (Giustozzi and Ali 2016, 5, 14). By contrast, during transition, the Afghans began diverging from the ISAF system by developing their own solutions and international advisers noted a more proactive mind-set in the force (Giustozzi and Kalinovsky 2016, 302). The shortcomings in the reform process lower the rating for the sustainability criterion, while positive trends have to be acknowledged as well. The Afghan government still lacks the financial resources needed for force sustainment, but it has increased its contributions over the last years (DOD 2017, 85). Despite the negative prediction by Krüger (2014, 40) that no serious reform efforts are ahead, President Ghani has initiated the Road Map plan that signals increasing commitment and ownership of the force and the security system beyond. Furthermore, the military doctrine which was simply exported from the U.S. is also currently under review (DOD 2017, 44). Therefore, the sustainability and ownership receives a level 3 rating (on its four-point scale) which signals that positive developments are very likely though significant challenges remain up to the date of this evaluation.

Coming to the next criterion, the previous sections raised concerns about the coherence of efforts, especially in view of its convoluted structure, e.g. criticized by Helmer (2008, 80-81). At least the army rebuilding did not have to struggle with coordination a dual programme like the police mission. Still, due to its multinational character, language and cultural barriers existed within the mission and between the advisers and the Afghans. In particular, the division of labour described for the training structure[53] proved difficult to merge when the forces joined their units. The confrontation of different military doctrines, training and methods was hardly workable (Giustozzi and Kalinovsky 2016, 253, 273). As there was no common understanding of

52 This uncovers the ambivalent perceptions of international advisers as negative impacts and perceptions of international advisers have already been described before, e.g. that some Afghans felt disrespected and wrongly treated (Giustozzi and Kalinovsky 2016, 263).

53 See section 4.3.1.

partnering and mentoring, coupled with a lack of clearly defined instructions, fragmentation between the participating nationalities persisted over time (ibid., 281). Furthermore, the rotation of staff in the advisory teams was identified a major challenge for institutional learning, the building of relationships to the Afghans, and the training schedule. The standardised ANA training cycle took nine months, whereas the OMLTs were deployed for six months and the ETTs for one year. The different durations lacked synchronisation resulting in a mismatch of the advising and deployment cycles (ibid., 274, 291, 314). In total, the organisational structure and execution of the mission fell short of acting in a joint and coherent fashion, even though the mission was not complicated by a separately running approach. The overall coherence of efforts proved unsatisfactory equating to a level 4 rating. This grade acknowledges the continuous attempts to improve and adapt the mission over the years (ibid., 280).

The coordination between the military reconstruction and other parts of the security system is hardly examined in studies about the mission. The low literacy of the force which is of concern up to today, signals that links between "soft" issues of developmental concern (such as educational support) and "hard" military issues (such as equipping the army) have been neglected in the past. SIGAR (2014, 15-16) on the other side noted increased cooperation between the UNESCO, the GIZ, the Afghan Ministry of Education, the MOI and MOD on the issue of literacy training, but oversight mechanisms to track the progress are lacking. Concerning the coordination between the police and the military, reports reveal, it was "so bad that on at least one occasion British forces, ANP and ANA ended up shooting at each other" (Giustozzi 2015, 203). Still in 2017, cross-pillar coordination between the two security forces remains a challenge (DOD 2017, 40). On the ministerial level, the coordination between the MOI and the MOD has been improved according to the U.S. DOD (2017, 87). Serious friction and communication issues between the two Afghan ministries undermined effective joined operations, yet the situation has reportedly improved over the years (Giustozzi 2015, 203). The friction and even violent clashes can be interpreted in a broader view as undermining efforts of peacebuilding and intra-Afghan reconciliation. To address the issue, President Ghani included the amelioration of inter-ministerial unity of command and effort in his Road Map reform (DOD 2017, 30).

Regarding another area of SSR, frequent allegations have been heard that ANA officers were involved in drug trafficking. The international coalition thus failed to forge links with anti-narcotics efforts headed by the United Kingdom (Giustozzi and Kalinovsky 2016, 266, Hammes 2015, 279). The forging and exploitation of ties between different parts of SSR has thus been insufficiently addressed, in particular in view of effective cross-pillar coordination on force and ministerial level. In view of the measures taken to enhance the situation, the coordination category is rated on a level 4 as the shortcomings and challenges currently dominate.

The last category reviews the promotion of values by the reconstruction mission. Concerning the mission itself, a contradiction between the formal guidelines and the actual implementation of measures can be noted. The mentoring guidelines recommended, among others, to let the Afghans discover and apply their own solution and to keep contact with the partnering units in daily routines (NATO 2013, 18-20). In reality, structures were modelled after Western templates (e.g. the MOD), and segregations, reservations and even mistrust dominated daily routines (Giustozzi and Kalinovsky 2016, 326, 333). The promotion of values within the army and the MOD was inhibited by wide-spread corruption and nepotism that also disrupt the chain of command (ibid., 265). The efforts of President Ghani to overhaul leadership address the common practice of patronage based appointments in the ANA and MOD (International Crisis Group 2017b, 15). At the same time, the very need to tackle this issue underlines the shortcomings in the promotion of good governance values by the international coalition. This is also underlined by reports about incidents when advisers tried to stop the physical abuse or killing of prisoners and were consequently threatened by the Afghan soldiers. Some internationals refrained from intervening as they feared for their lives (Giustozzi and Kalinovsky 2016, 321-322). As in the case of the police, the GAO and SIGAR reports illustrate that the rebuilding was tried to be executed in accordance with the principles of transparency and accountability, but their limitations have already been noted above. Nevertheless, the public view of the army stands out positively in comparison to the police. Accusations of human rights abuses by ANA soldiers have been heard more often since the security transition, but such incidences are described as exceptional (Giustozzi 2015, 204-205). Consequently, the reform's consistency with values presents overall unsatisfactory results which equates to a level 4 rating. The generally positive reputation, in addition to the reform efforts in leadership are discernible positive results, despite the numerous persistent shortfalls in principles and values of security governance.

Putting all categories of the assessment framework together, the average rating for the ANA reconstruction mission is 3.75. This score underlines that the results are largely satisfactory with a negative tendency. In contrast to the police reform whose overall rating was 4.25, the international efforts for military reconstruction have performed slightly better. As an illustration of the ratings, figure 5 demonstrates the remarkable inefficiency of the mission as its most striking drawback.

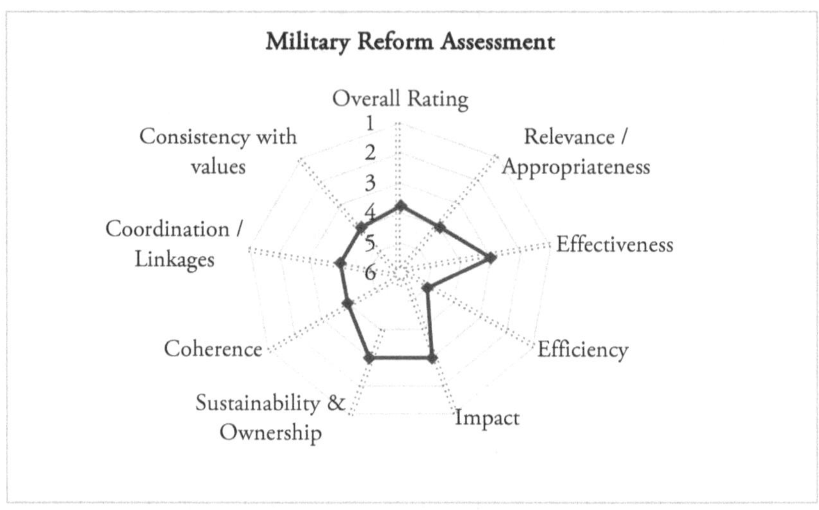

Figure 5: Military Reform Rating (Source: own figure)

In consideration of the several mispurchases and the convoluted mission structure, the study calls for enhanced pre-decision planning and assessment, in addition to a streamlining of command-structures (Helmer 2008, 81). Reviewing the original targets, the ANA has exceeded the target size of 70,000 forces by more than double, but it lags behind the current target of 195,000 forces (U.S. GAO 2005, 6, DOD 2017, 51). The army is increasingly ethnically balanced, but Tajiks are still over-represented in the force. Besides, ethnic-balancing was raised as a challenge to merit based appointments which also applies to the ANP (Giustozzi 2015, 139-140). Other reform targets were loyalty, discipline, professionalization, affordability and sustainability (Giustozzi and Kalinovsky 2016, 239). In all these issues, improvements are observable over the years. However, considerable shortcomings have also been uncovered. In January 2016 President Ghani declared the abolition of penalties for deserters if they return to the army within six months – revealing the difficulties concerning loyalty and discipline (Schetter and Mielke 2016, 636). The Afghan government remains dependent on donor support in order to fund the army (and the police) and educate high numbers of fresh recruits due to grave attrition rates. This in turn indicates persistent challenges in the sustainability and professionalization. Therefore, the original targets cannot be regarded as achieved by 2017. Despite these flaws, the positive reputation of the ANA has to be emphasised, in particular in contrast to the police (Giustozzi 2015, 204-205).

4.4. Lessons Learned about SSR and State-Building in Afghanistan

After analysing the police and military reconstruction, this section merges the findings with regards to our initial research question on the contribution of security sector reform on state-building in Afghanistan. In contrast to the conclusion of the overall research process provided in the next chapter, this section pays special attention on the lessons learned from our case study. At this point, the results are discussed in relation to previous research and interpretations in order to critically evaluate our study.

As a starting point, Hammes (2015, 277) noted that security has become a centre of gravity for international state-building efforts. The review of both processes confirmed this statement by uncovering the heavy investments made by the international community, in particular the USA, for the Afghan security sector. SIGAR (2017, 87) published that as of 30 June 2017, more than 61.4 percent of all U.S. funding for Afghanistan since 2002 was for the Afghan security forces, which is more than $73.5 billion. This number illustrates the "securitization"[54] of the state-building programme in the country, especially under the U.S. flag. Additionally, it underlines that "soft" developmental issues have been of second-order to funding state-building in the country. The persistent gap in the recruitment of literate personnel in the ANP and ANA requires the forging of security and development links. Actually, the OECD (2008, 13) calls for an implementation of SSR that integrates security and development policies in recognition of the so-called "security-development nexus" as mentioned in section 2.3. The lack in key reading skills of the recruits was only integrated after seven years of international reconstruction in the country between 2009 and 2010 as a key part of SSR (Hammes 2015, 288). However, the programme turned out to be of questionable quality, while the pervasive illiteracy in the ANDSF impedes their effectiveness and sustainability up till today (Katzman and Thomas 2017, 32, SIGAR 2014, 16-17).

At the outset of the study, it was emphasised that the military and the police are two distinct security providers whose reconstruction was organised in a division of labour by the lead nation concept (Hammes 2015, 279). During the analysis, it has become clear that the lead nation concept failed

[54] See section 2.3.

for the ANP's reconstruction as the USA de facto headed the process by introducing its own model of training and mentoring, and outdoing the German approach in terms of funding and staffing. The U.S. leadership in both rebuilding agendas has, however, not translated into a coherent approach (Giustozzi and Kalinovsky 2016, 241). Quite the contrary, the operation's organisation was criticised as convoluted and overly complex, which inhibited a timely execution of tasks (Helmer 2008, 80). For police reconstruction, the situation was even more compounded by the dual programmes of the Europeans (Germany and later the EU) and the U.S.-Americans – visible in the lower level 5 score for coherence in the ANP's reconstruction in contrast to a (still low) level 4 rating of the ANA's process (see figure 3 & 5). Thus, the organisational and programmatic execution of both reconstruction processes is at odds with the OECD's "Principles for Good International Engagement" that stipulate joint, coordinated and integrated engagement between international actors (OECD 2007, 3 p.8).

As noted before, there is "a consensus among observers that building up the ANA worked out much better than the corresponding effort to develop the ANP" (Giustozzi and Kalinovsky 2016, 292). The average ratings for the ANA reconstruction of 3.75 and for the ANP of 4.25 generally confirm this statement.[55] However, the difference in the numbers and the persistent weaknesses of the ANA presented above do not confirm the accentuation of "much better". There is hardly any reason given for the better performance, but simply stated that "the military organisation dedicated to the task was more comfortable dealing with another military organisation (the Afghan MoD) than with the Afghan MoI" (ibid.).

The analysis of the reconstruction programmes in this study, on the other hand, points out three main reasons for the divergence in the reconstruction performance: the aforementioned dual agenda that hampered the complementarity of measures, the disagreements within the coalition to balance counterinsurgency with other policing tasks, and the ambivalent impact of the ALP. Referring to the second point, the disunity in the coalition resulted in an overemphasis of counterinsurgency involvement of the police while neglecting civil policing tasks such as criminal prosecution (DOD 2017, 76). In theory, the police are assigned the task of managing small-scale violence in a society, i.e. enforcing law and order to support (and execute) the state's monopoly on the legitimate use of force in a Weberian sense. The military is assigned the task and capacities to manage large-scale violence in terms of operating in large formations or having the heavy equipment to fulfil this task in contrast to the police (Giustozzi and Isaqzadeh 2013, 3-5). Although

55 See section 4.2.3 for the police rating and 4.3.3 for the military assessment.

this is an ideal type description of these institutions, the unclear assignment of tasks and the police's heavy involvement in counterinsurgency, hence managing large-scale violence without suitable equipment and training resulted in the observed capacity gaps and higher casualty rates than the army (Hammes 2015, 296). This beats back on the overall authority and legitimacy of the Afghan state, as well as the very need to establish the Afghan Local Police. In the embattled areas of Helmand and Kandahar, the military proved able to recapture insurgent provinces, but the police failed to fill effectively the power vacuum resulting in fragile government authority or a reoccupation by the Taliban or other insurgent groups (Krüger 2014, 84). As of May 2017, almost 30 percent of Afghanistan's districts were contested areas, 11 percent were under insurgent control or influence, and less than 60 percent under government control or influence of which the NUG effectively controls less than 24 percent (SIGAR 2017, 88). In comparison to the same period in 2016, these numbers illustrate a decline in government authority over territory with a more than two-percent increase of insurgent-dominated districts (ibid.).

Concerning the ambivalent role of the ALP, it was created as a remedy for lacking governmental authority in remote areas hazarding the consequences of impeding DDR-programmes and enabling forces of questionable loyalty and documented criminal behaviour (Katzman and Thomas 2017, 36-37, Hammes 2015, 299). Co-opting non-state providers of security is indeed included in the security reform guidelines provided by the World Bank (2012, 26). Yet they also stress the accountability of security forces and measures to rein in human rights abuses, so that the state's legitimacy is strengthened and promoted (ibid.). The mixed-record of the ALP undermines these aspects. Although the establishment and performance of the force has been repeatedly criticized e.g. by Hammes (2015, 299), there is hardly any lessons learned or recommendations offered concerning the local forces. The study has shown that the MOI is increasingly working on registering the ALP in AHRIMS, which will provide greater oversight and accountability of this branch (SIGAR 2017, 104). This is in line with the recommendation by Giustozzi and Isagzadeh (2013, 64) to create stricter supervision. Yet, they also state that this requires a more capable central bureaucracy, which the MOI failed to develop (ibid.). Still in 2017, the MoI and its ANP is staying behind the MOD and its ANA in development and performance (DOD 2017, 42, 70, 76). However, this study also reported significant progress in the establishment of AHRIMS in both the MOI and the MOD (SIGAR 2017, 102-103). Therefore, the evaluation results draw a more optimistic picture concerning the capacities of the Afghan central government, in particular the MOI, than other studies, e.g. provided by Schetter and Mielke (2016, 637). A further indication of this assessment is President Ghani's Road Map reform that signals discernible progress in state-building after the termination of the large-scale ISAF. It also confirms the findings that Afghanistan's government has generally increased its capacity since 2001 and that the NUG under President Ghani has taken an active role in further reforming the country despite its internal tensions (Katzman and Thomas 2017, 9). The Bertelsmann Transformation Index underlines Ghani's positive reputation among Afghans as a "visionary" (Bertelsmann Stiftung 2016, 24). In the time series, the index reveals that Afghanistan has been on the last ranks of "hard-line autocracy" signalling failed transformation since the beginning of record in 2006 (Bertelsmann Stiftung 2017). The stateness score increased from 3,0 in 2006 to 3,8 in 2016, but stays in the second lowest category ("flawed"). Other indicators such as rule of law (2006: 2,3; 2016: 2,5 raised to the bottom line of "flawed"), political and social integration (2006: 2,3; 2016: 2,3 equating to the lowest "poor performance" category) do not follow this positive trend, or even decline such as political participation (2006: 4,3; 2016: 3,5 meaning "flawed").[56] The latest index of 2016 was published in the second year of Ghani's term. Thus, it does not reflect the latest reform efforts whose impact has to be observed in the upcoming years. The index scores are therefore more in line with Schetter and Mielke (2016, 637) who note growing repressive policies subverting liberal reform approaches.

Indeed, the observed progress cannot whitewash the significant shortcomings of the SSR process and current capability gaps in the ANDSF. The loss of territorial control may turn out a warning sign of setbacks in state-building. Even worse, Krüger (2014) attests the ANDSF a "process of decay" (86) due to high attrition and low retention rates. Giustozzi and Ali (2016) report about – yet unverified – rumours that the ANA is "on the verge of collapse" (15). The development of both the ANA and the ANP has proven to be increasingly difficult to oversee confirming the finding that the situation is hardly verifiable. With the start of transition, foreign personnel assigned for monitoring the capabilities has also been withdrawn leaving the international side dependent on the reports of the Afghan authorities. The current RS mission has only little or no direct contact to ANDSF forces below regional commands – for the ANA below corps level, and for ANP below

[56] The score for political participation has increased slightly since 2014 (then 3,3) (Bertelsmann Stiftung 2017).

zone-headquarters level. The Afghan records are thus accepted without independent verification despite a lack of quality detected in the provided assessments (SIGAR 2017, 97). While prior capability assessments were of questionable reliability and sustainability too, they did at least track the progress of the ANDSF over time in order to provide some transparency and data usable for evaluations (Sopko 2016, 9). The last unit based assessments have been reported for the year 2013, which makes the data stale in view of the backsliding of capabilities in the past and turnover of the troops' composition (SIGAR 2014a, 5). The international community was aware of this problem; in 2014, SIGAR warned of declining monitoring capabilities (ibid., 11). For political stakeholders and donors, this poses the threat of making decisions based on faulty assessments, while for scholars and the public, the situation and actions of their representatives become increasingly difficult to appraise. State-building is described as an inherently complex task and challenging to study.[57] The decreasing insights into the process in Afghanistan have further impeded in-depths assessments. Figuratively speaking, the transition of security responsibility and withdrawal of international staff was like closing the "black box" of the Afghan state with a lid for external research.

The overall evolution of the state-building approach of the international coalition in Afghanistan features a significant value gap apparent in the antithesis between the language of guidelines and the actual measures implemented in the country (Giustozzi and Kalinovsky 2016, 334). For example, the OECD's handbook on SSR stresses the importance of context-sensitive reform approaches based on local ownership of the reform process (OECD 2008, 30-32). The international programme in Afghanistan, on the contrary, implemented copy-and-paste templates for the military doctrine, the ministries, and the logistical system (Giustozzi and Kalinovsky 2016, 333-335). These were applied out of practical necessity, as the state-building approach did not rely on years of planning. However, their unsuitability for the Afghan context resulted in limited capacities of the ANDSF, hence the government in the areas concerned (ibid., 335, 338). The continuous adaption of security reconstruction and training programmes demonstrate a "learning by doing"-approach to state-building which finally resulted in embracing a "good enough"-attitude (ibid., 337). This is visible in the ISAF Guide that emphasises: "Better that the Afghans do something adequately than we do it perfectly" (NATO 2013, 19). This in turn led to a more proactive Afghan force developing their own, albeit imperfect ways of handling its daily routines (Giustozzi and Kalinovsky 2016, 302).

---

57 Referring to section 2.4.

Another central value to any international intervention has been the principle to "do no harm" (OECD 2007, 1 p.2). For SSR, this implies to consider the trade-offs between enabling the institutions to exert violence and their broader impact on the dynamics of conflict (OECD 2010, 89). In studies about SSR in Afghanistan critical issues were observed, but not related to this imperative of engagement. Among others, the impact of the ALP in crime and human rights abuses, the (illegal) selling of police or military equipment risking to fuel insurgency and undermine DDR measures, and ultimately the resentments of Afghan forces caused by inadequate training measures have been noted in the previous sections. These examples of "harm" caused by the SSR mission underline the importance of context-sensitive planning and implementing oversight mechanisms in recognition of potential risks and trade-offs. Both have been repeatedly found to be lacking in the execution of the reconstruction mission, which again hints for a value gap between the guidelines and the implementation of the mission.

The review of the reconstruction processes has revealed that the major flaws of the mission (e.g. persistent understaffing, the neglect of judiciary reform, and the lack of an overarching strategy) were recognised at an early stage (U.S. GAO 2005, 14-15, 29). This confirms the statement of Hammes (2015, 290) that failings were known, but the NATO had been unable to address them. The repeated changes in plan are of Janus-faced character, as they do not only demonstrate, in a positive notion, the adaptiveness of the process, but also the lack of overarching, long-term strategies (Sedra 2007, 170). Remembering the findings of section 2.2.1, transformation of political institutions is a painfully slow process taking generations, so that the World Bank cautions to "not expect too much, too soon" (World Bank 2011, 108). In view of the constant changes of plan in Afghanistan, the actual impact of measures seems hard to gauge as plans were discarded as ineffective after a short time span.

Summarising the evaluation results concerning the three dimensions of state-building (authority, capacity, legitimacy)[58]applicable to the security domain, the process remains incomplete as persistent challenges have been revealed. Insurgent forces keep challenging government authority and the strengthening of the monopoly on the legitimate use of force. The Afghan government is currently not able to provide for security within its territory. Even worse, pro-government forces have been identified as a cause for civilian casualties and human rights abuses (UNAMA 2017, 94-96). This deprives the government of popular loyalty, hence state legitimacy as emphasised in section 2.1.2 about core functions of the state (OECD 2010, 88).

[58] Referring to section 3.2.

The Taliban are still able to install and maintain shadow administration structures in their controlled districts that impede central government authority (Ruttig 2016, 118). Furthermore, the NUG remains dependent on foreign support to uphold and enforce their authority in embattled areas. The persistent donor dependency of the Afghan state also refers to the capacity dimension regarding lacking financial sustainability[59] and noticeable gaps in key skills of the ANDSF (Ruttig 2015). However, in all three key dimensions, the support provided through SSR measures resulted in improvements and ongoing reform efforts. President Ghani's Road Map demonstrates increased Afghan ownership of the reform efforts. Though partisanship, corruption and internal disagreements permeate the NUG and all levels of the security sector, political willingness to address these issues is visible in the reassignment of leadership posts starting in early 2017 (SIGAR 2017, 94-95). At the same time, resistance against the reform has been noted as e.g. anti-corruption plans and redeployment result in power losses of current profiteers on all levels of the system (International Crisis Group 2017b, i).

For a better illustration of the findings, the following figure sums up the core results about the state-building progress (figure 6). Based on the analysis of the police and military reconstruction process, the points presented refer particularly to the security domain, thus they remain limited in their scope. Nonetheless, they provide an overview of the key contributions of SSR to the current status of state-building in Afghanistan.

Despite the shortcomings of the international reconstruction agenda and continuing weaknesses of the Afghan security system and the state in general, it has to be stressed that the entry point for reform was starting from shambles. Entire governance structures and personnel had to be created from the remnants of war and the authoritarian rule of the Taliban. Being fully aware of the shortfalls of the reconstruction process and current status, to raise more than 350.000 security forces and establishing training and administration structures including the ministries, is an undeniable success of the international and local state-building efforts. As Hammes (2015) points out, "these are truly remarkable accomplishments" (277-278). The main challenge of state-building in Afghanistan has thus not been to create, but to sustain and enhance the achievements. This in turn relates back to the imbalance between quality and quantity of the reconstruction approach (Sedra 2010,

[59] Donor support has contributed the majority of Afghanistan's national budget, though there is a tendency of increased national capability. While the donor funding made up around 70 percent of the national budget in 2013-2014, in the current fiscal year 1396, the contribution is estimated at 62 percent (SIGAR 2017, 161, Bertelsmann Stiftung 2016, 4). This number still underlines Afghanistan's heavy aid dependency.

236). The repeated backsliding of capabilities in the ANDSF and heavy donor dependency of the Afghan state are only two manifestations of fragile accomplishments by SSR in the framework of state-building.

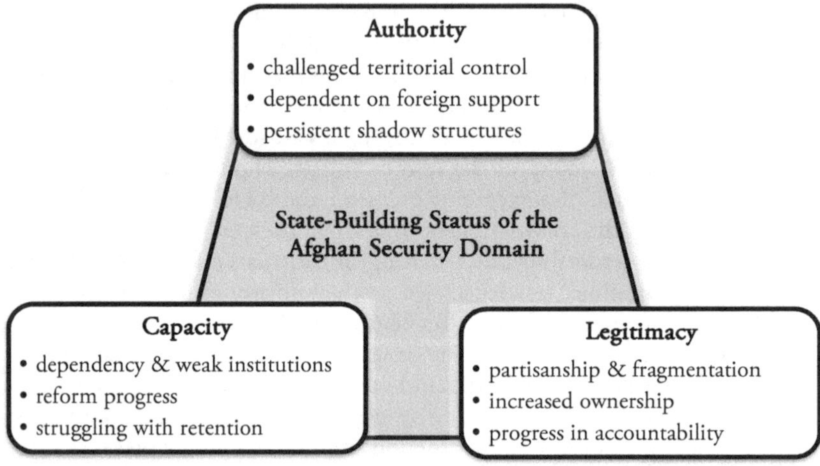

Figure 6: State-Building Status of the Afghan Security Domain (Source: own figure)

5. Conclusion: Digging into Chaos

After more than 15 years of international intervention in Afghanistan, the Afghan state is still challenged by internal strife resulting in the death and displacement of thousands of its people every year. Even worse, civilian casualties have been on the rise with 2016 being the most violent year since UNAMA started recording these tolls in 2009 (UNAMA 2017, 3-5). The Afghan state is unable to guarantee the security of its inhabitants, calling into question the overall impact of international efforts to re-build the Afghan state and its security system. Therefore, the study aimed to identify the contribution of security sector reconstruction to state-building in Afghanistan.

As a first step, this required to understand the fundamentals of the state, state-building and the role of security. This theoretical review has revealed the lack of conceptual clarity of the state, its requirements and key features, which translate into the disagreements about the chances of state-building. The academic dispute is apparent in the clash between state-building proponents and opponents arguing about the very possibility of purposeful state-building and beyond about the role of externals to administer this process (Debiel and Rinck 2017, 404). Despite these elementary controversies, in international politics state-building has evolved into a common practice for countering fragility and its negative fallouts such as terrorism (Fukuyama 2005, xvii).

Based on the Weberian model of a bureaucratised state, state-building is an inherently Western and normative conception with security as a core function needed to gain stability and legitimacy (Sisk 2013, 54-55). Yet the very definition of legitimacy remains a controversial issue (Eabrasu 2012, 207-208). Therefore, already the initial chapters of the study illustrated the unresolved controversies about the ubiquitous cornerstone of political sciences and the world order itself: the state. While the state and state-building are contested subjects, there are currently no coherent and comprehensive conceptual alternatives to them (Debiel and Rinck 2017, 410, Fukuyama 2005,

162). The continuous debate about the concepts has contributed to their evolution and further improvements, which has been uncovered in comparison to peace-building and nation-building in section 2.2.2. This also reflects the adaption of the reconstruction process in Afghanistan.

The mixed record of state-building approaches in Afghanistan and other countries has led to an increasing disillusionment among the international practitioners of state-building – in particular the USA (Debiel and Rinck 2017, 404, Hammes 2015, 303). In view of currently lacking alternatives, as well as empirical evidence that weak states, not sophisticated states, provide the breeding ground for international hazards, the main task of research is to ameliorate current approaches by identifying best practices or developing new ones (Hirschmann 2016, 48-51). In the words of Francis Fukuyama (2005, 163): "Learning to do state-building better is thus central to the future of world order."

The multidimensional character of the state and the complex interrelatedness of policy issues, however, compound this task. Taking a closer look at state-building evaluations, this manifests in the absence of comparative analysis and methodological frameworks. Therefore, the study merged existing evaluation criteria and qualitative analysis in a framework[60] that may be applied to other environments in future research. The criteria for evaluation are based on the OECD's guidelines for SSR (OECD 2008, 241-242, 2011b, 48-50). To operationalize these criteria, the KfW's rating levels have been applied, although the institution itself only evaluates the original five criteria of state-building.[61] The diverging rating scales with sustainability the only category to apply a four-point scale are difficult to compare and merge. A task for the KfW or related future research is therefore to develop a sophisticated, comprehensible and comparable rating scheme for all categories, which this study could not provide due to its limited scope.

In order to gauge the impact of SSR on state-building, the analysis merged the sectoral studies and the dimensions provided by the World Bank – authority, capacity and legitimacy (World Bank 2012, 26). Although this sounds like a piecemeal approach, the framework acknowledges the multiple facets of SSR and structures the analysis towards the overarching state-building agenda. It facilitates the comparison between different programmes such as the police and the military reconstruction, and offers the opportunity to expand and even transfer the analysis framework on other areas of state-build-

60 Referring to section 3.

61 These criteria are relevance, effectiveness, impact, efficiency and sustainability (KfW 2017).

ing (e.g. the education system). Nevertheless, certain caveats have been explored that need to be taken into consideration for future research. First, the evaluation criteria overlap, thus certain points are applicable to several categories at once. For example, the high attrition rate of the forces hampered their sustainability and effectiveness at the same time. Secondly, the rating levels are highly dependent on the researcher's qualitative judgement. Two main reasons cause this complication: lacking quantitative data in conflict-affected countries and the fuzzy thresholds between the rating levels. The first is directly related to the destructive nature of war making it hard to resolve; the second is only affected by missing research. Future studies may thus concentrate on clarifying and streamlining the rating system in order to facilitate inter-state comparisons. With this, the analysis on the contribution of SSR on state-building in Afghanistan offers a first concept to fill the gap of comparative studies stressed by Debiel and Rinck (2017, 412).

Referring back to the research question, what security sector reconstruction contributes to state-building in Afghanistan, the first and foremost result sounds obvious: it contributes a bulk of financial, material and personnel resources (Bertelsmann Stiftung 2016, 3). Secondly, it has resulted in a "Westernization" of the Afghan security system apparent in the structure of the forces, the ministries, and their management systems (Giustozzi and Kalinovsky 2016, 338-340). Thirdly, it has promoted – though insufficiently – the Afghan's government monopoly on the use of legitimate force by creating the institutions to manage small- and large scale violence.

This, in turn, leads to what SSR did not contribute to the overall state-building process. Most importantly, SSR turned out not to be the panacea for Afghanistan's fragility, it was expected to be (Sedra 2007, 160). Referred to as the "ticket home" (Hammes 2015, 277), the efforts failed to achieve their initial goals to create mature ANDSF both in quantity and quality. Instead, the engagement had to be prolonged several times and due to a deterioration of the security situation even intensified in resources and personnel. The termination of the large-scale ISAF mission cannot be equated to "the end of the war" (Otłowski 2014, 2), but to an end of in-depth insights into the capacities of the Afghan state and its forces. This further complicates an up-to-date assessment of SSR in Afghanistan, as for example unit capabilities are no more publicly reported. The latest decision to reinforce international troops illustrates the imperfection and incompleteness of SSR and state-building in the country (Holland and Walcott 2017). It is important to realise that the deficiencies of SSR in Afghanistan recoiled not only on the mission's structure, but also on the self-perception of the actors involved and their state-building approach. This is illustrated by the speech of U.S. President Donald Trump on 21 August 2017 in which he called the intervention in Afghanistan a "war without victory" and rejected future nation-building in the country (The New York Times 2017).

By and large, the involvement in security system reconstruction in Afghanistan has led to the ultimate recognition that "security forces are essential but insufficient" (Hammes 2015, 325) to provide for sustainable state-building. The process is still incomplete and, with respect to the caution issued by the World Bank, will still need some time to transform the Afghan state from fragility to resilience (World Bank 2011, 108). Researchers, stakeholders and the public are well advised to consider the World Bank's warning when trying to assess the impact of the mission, planning future involvement, or discarding state-building measures as useless. Fragility and thus the demand for state-building has been observed as increasing rather than diminishing on the international agenda (Krause and Mallory 2010, 1). This again requires a refocused research agenda that does not only criticize the failure of state-building (e.g. Groß and Grimm 2016), but reversely asks for the conditions of its success. Its potential is visible in the evolution of state-building conceptions and practices, which have contributed to the adaption of international efforts in Afghanistan and beyond. The study has revealed that state-building means, for practitioners and researchers alike, to dig into the chaos of conflict, history and society. Digging into such chaos and unravelling its dynamics has, to put it bluntly, the potential to shape the future of the state and thus tomorrow's world order.

Literature

Acemoglu, D., & Robinson, J. A. (2013). *Why Nations Fail: The Origins of Power, Prosperity, and Poverty* (First published in 2012 ed.). London: Profile Books LTD.

Afghanistan Research and Evaluation Unit (AREU). (2017). *About Afghanistan Research and Evaluation Unit (AREU).* Retrieved April 25, 2017, from Afghanistan Research and Evaluation Unit: Research for a Better Afghanistan: https://areu.org.af/about-us

Ansary, T. (2012). *Games without Rules.* Philadelphia: PublicAffairs.

Barton, F. D. (2010). Measuring Progress in International State-Building and Reconstruction. In J. Krause, & C. K. IV (Eds.), *International State Building and Reconstruction Efforts: Experience Gained and Lessons Learned* (pp. 17-32). Opladen & Farminton Hills, MI: Barbara Budrich Publishers.

Berger, M. T. (2006, August 08). From nation-building to state-building: The geopolitics of development, the nation-state system and the changing global order. *Third World Quarterly*, pp. 5-25.

Bertelsmann Stiftung. (2016). *BTI 2016 - Afghanistan Country Report.* Retrieved April 23, 2017, from Bertelsmann Stiftung: https://www.bti-project.org/fileadmin/files/BTI/Downloads/Reports/2016/pdf/BTI_2016_Afghanistan.pdf

Bertelsmann Stiftung. (2017). *Transformation Index BTI 2016.* Retrieved October 24, 2017, from https://www.bti-project.org/en/reports/country-reports/detail/itc/afg/itr/aso/

Blatter, J. K., Janning, F., & Wagemann, C. (2007). *Qualitative Politikanalyse: eine Einführung in Forschungsansätze und Methoden.* Wiesbaden: VS Verlag für Sozialwissenschaften.

Call, C. T., & Cousens, E. M. (2008). Ending wars and building peace: International responses to war-torn societies. *International Studies Perspectives, 9*(1), pp. 1-21.

Caplan, R. (2005). *International Governance of War-Torn Territories: Rule and Reconstruction.* Oxford, New York: Oxford University Press.

Collier, P., Elliott, V. L., Hegre, H., Hoeffler, A., Reynal-Querol, M., & Sambanis, N. (2003). *Breaking the Conflict Trap : Civil War and Development Policy. A World Bank policy research report.* Washington, DC: World Bank and Oxford University Press.

Cordesman, A. H., & Lin, A. (2015). *Afghanistan at Transition: Lessons of the Longest War.* Washington, D.C.: Center for Strategic and International Studies.

Costantini, I. (2015, January 09). *Statebuilding versus state formation: the political economy of transition in Iraq and Libya.* Retrieved June 08, 2017, from PhD thesis, University of Trento: http://eprints-phd.biblio.unitn.it/1519/1/Costantini_dissertation_deposit.pdf

Debiel, T., & Reinhardt, D. (2004). Staatsverfall und Weltordnungspolitik: analytische Zugänge und politische Strategien zu Beginn des 21. Jahrhunderts. *Nord-Süd aktuell, 18*(3), pp. 525-536.

Debiel, T., & Rinck, P. (2017). Statebuilding. In M. Dunn Cavelty, & T. Balzacq (Eds.), *Routledge handbook of security studies* (pp. 404-414). London; New York: Routledge, Taylor & Francis Group.

Deutsche Gesellschaft für Internationale Zusammenarbeit (GIZ) GmbH. (2015, August). *Measuring Results, Contributing to Results: Findings and conclusions from monitoring and evaluation 2012-2014.* Bonn: Deutsche Gesellschaft für Internationale Zusammenarbeit (GIZ) GmbH. Retrieved from https://www.giz.de/de/downloads/giz2016-en-monitoring.pdf

Eabrasu, M. (2012). Les états de la définition wébérienne de l'État. *Raisons politiques, 1*(No. 45), pp. 187-209.

Eriksen, S. S. (2016, August 05). *State effects and the effects of state building: institution building and the formation of state-centred societies.* Retrieved from Third World Quarterly: DOI: 10.1080/01436597.2016.1176854

Fukuyama, F. (2005). *State-Building: Governance and World Order in the Twenty-First Century* (paperback edition of the 2004 published edition ed.). London: Profile Books LTD.

Ghani, A., & Lockhart, C. (2010). Lessons Unlearned: Why Most International Reconstruction Efforts in the Past Have Failed. In J. Krause, & C. K. IV (Eds.), *International State Building and Reconstruction Efforts: Experience Gained and Lessons Learned* (pp. 5-16). Opladen & Farminton Hills, MI: Barbara Budrich Publishers.

Giustozzi, A. (2015). *The Army of Afghanistan: A Political History of a Fragile Institution.* London: Hurst Publishers.

Giustozzi, A., & Ali, A. M. (2016, March). *The Afghan National Army After ISAF.* Retrieved August 25, 2017, from Afghan Research and Evaluation Unit (AREU): https://areu.org.af/wp-content/uploads/2016/03/1603E-The-Afghan-National-Army-after-ISAF.pdf

Giustozzi, A., & Isaqzadeh, M. (2013). *Policing Afghanistan.* London: Hurst Publishers.

Giustozzi, A., & Kalinovsky, A. M. (2016). *Missionaries of Modernity: Advisory Missions and the Struggle for Hegemony in Afghanistan and Beyond.* London: Hurst Publishers.

Grävingholt, J., Gänzle, S., & Ziaja, S. (2009). *The convergence of peacebuilding and state building: addressing a common purpose from different perspectives.* Retrieved June 06, 2017, from Deutsches Institut für Entwicklungspolitik (DIE): https://www.die-gdi.de/uploads/media/BP_4.2009.pdf

Grenier, S. M. (2015). Introduction: Framing the War in Afghanistan. In G. A. Mattox, & S. M. Grenier (Eds.), *Coalition Challenges in Afghanistan: The Politics of Alliance* (pp. 1-12). Stanford: Stanford University Press.

Grindle, M. S. (2004). Good Enough Governance: Poverty Reduction and Reform in Developing Countries. *Governance: An International Journal of Policy, Administration, and Institutions, 4*(17), pp. 525-548.

Groß, L., & Grimm, S. (2016, March 10). Conflicts of preferences and domestic constraints: understanding reform failure in liberal state-building and democracy promotion. *Contemporary Politics*, pp. 1-19.

Hammes, T. X. (2015). Raising and Mentoring Security Forces in Afghanistan and Iraq. In R. D. Hooker, & J. J. Collins (Eds.), *Lessons Encountered: Learning from the Long War* (pp. 277-344). Washington, DC: National Defense University Press.

Hänggi, H. (2010). Establishing Security in Conflict-Affected Societies: How to Reform the Security Sector. In J. Krause, & C. K. IV (Eds.), *International State Building and Reconstruction Efforts: Experience Gained and Lessons Learned* (pp. 77-97). Opladen & Farminton Hills, MI: Barbara Budrich Publishers.

Harooni, M. (2017, May 09). *Afghan forces try to push back Taliban from Kunduz city.* (T. Heneghan, Ed.) Retrieved May 15, 2017, from Reuters: http://www.reuters.com/article/us-afghanistan-taliban-idUSKBN1851WN

Helmer, D. (2008, July-August). Twelve urgent steps for the Advisor Mission in Afghanistan. *Military Review*, pp. 73-81.

Hirschmann, K. (2016). *Wie Staaten schwach werden: Fragilität von Staaten als internationale Herausforderung.* Bonn: Bundeszentrale für politische Bildung (bpb).

Hobbes, T. (1894). *Leviathan; or, The matter, form, and power of a commonwealth ecclesiastical and civil* (4th ed.). (H. Morley, Ed.) London, Glasgow, New York: G. Routledge and Sons.

Holland, S., & Walcott, J. (2017, August 03). *Insider - Trumps Top-Berater nach Afghanistan-Beratungen "fassungslos".* Retrieved August 09, 2017, from Reuters: http://de.reuters.com/article/afghanistan-usa-trump-idDEKBN1AJ0G9

Hughes, M. (2014, May). *The Afghan National Police in 2015 and Beyond.* Retrieved August 08, 2017, from United States Institut of Peace (USIP) - Special Report 346: https://www.usip.org/sites/default/files/SR346_The_Afghan_National_Police_in_2015_and_Beyond.pdf

International Crisis Group. (2017a, April 27). *Watch List 2017. First Update.* Retrieved May 05, 2017, from International Crisis Group:

https://d2071andvip0wj.cloudfront.net/WL%202017-Update%201%20(1).pdf

International Crisis Group. (2017b, April 10). *Afghanistan: The Future of the National Unity Government. Asia Report N°285.* Retrieved August 15, 2017, from International Crisis Group: https://d2071andvip0wj.cloudfront.net/285-afghanistan-the-future-of-the-national-unity-government%20(1).pdf

Jellinek, G., & Jellinek, W. (1914). *Allgemeine Staatslehre* (3rd ed.). Berlin: Verlag von O. Häring.

Katzman, K., & Thomas, C. (2017, August 22). *Afghanistan: Post-Taliban Governance, Security, and U.S. Policy.* Retrieved August 27, 2017, from Congressional Research Service (RL30588): https://fas.org/sgp/crs/row/RL30588.pdf

KfW. (2015). *Ex post evaluation – Afghanistan: City Network Rehabilitation Kabul.* Retrieved July 30, 2017, from KfW Development Bank: https://www.kfw-entwicklungsbank.de/PDF/Evaluierung/Ergebnisse-und-Publikationen/PDF-Dokumente-A-D_EN/Afghanistan_Stadtnetz_Kabul_2015_E.pdf

KfW. (2017). *Evaluation Criteria.* Retrieved June 26, 2017, from KfW Development Bank: https://www.kfw-entwicklungsbank.de/International-financing/KfW-Development-Bank/Evaluations/Evaluation-criteria/

Knopf, J. W. (2004, August 08). Did Reagan Win the Cold War? *Strategic Insights*(3 (8)), p. http://hdl.handle.net/10945/11247.

Krause, J. (2010). The Future of International State-Building and Reconstruction Efforts: Summary and Recommendations. In J. Krause, & C. K. IV (Eds.), *International State Building and Reconstruction Efforts: Experience Gained and Lessons Learned* (pp. 157-171). Opladen & Farminton Hills, MI: Barbara Budrich Publishers.

Krause, J., & Mallory, C. K. (2010). Introduction. In J. Krause, & C. K. IV (Eds.), *International State Building and Reconstruction Efforts: Experience Gained and Lessons Learned* (pp. 1-4). Opladen & Farminton Hills, MI: Barbara Budrich Publishers.

Krüger, U. (2014). *Schadensfall Afghanistan.* Bonn: Bouvier Verlag.

Lee, G. (2012). *Fighting Season: Tales of a British Officer in Afghanistan* (International Edition ed.). London: Duckworth Publishing.

Mackenzie, J. (2017, April 28). *Afghan Taliban launch spring offensive as U.S. reviews strategy.* (M. Perry, Ed.) Retrieved May 15, 2017, from Reuters: http://www.reuters.com/article/us-afghanistan-taliban-idUSKBN17U0E9

Mattox, G. A. (2015). Going Forward: Lessons Learned. In G. A. Mattox, & S. M. Grenier (Eds.), *Coalition Challenges in Afghanistan: The Politics of Alliance* (pp. 288-304). Stanford: Stanford University Press.

Mayer-Rieckh, A. (2013). *Dealing with the Past in Security Sector Reform.* (H. Hänggi, & A. Schnabel, Eds.) Geneva: The Geneva Centre for the Democratic Control of Armed Forces (DCAF).

Murray, T. (2007). Police-Building in Afghanistan: A Case Study of Civil Security Reform. *International Peacekeeping, 14*(1), pp. 108-126. doi:http://dx.doi.org/10.1080/13533310601114327

Murray, T. (2011, January 01). Security Sector Reform in Afghanistan, 2002–2011: An Overview of a Flawed Process. *International Studies, 48*(1), pp. 43-63. doi:10.1177/002088171204800103

NATO. (2013). *ISAF Security Force Assistance Guide.* International Security Assistance Forces (ISAF) and the Security Force Assistance (SFA). Retrieved from https://info.publicintelligence.net/ISAF-SecurityForceAssistance.pdf

NATO. (2016, July 09). Warsaw Summit Declaration on Afghanistan. Issued by the Heads of State and Government of Afghanistan and Allies and their Resolute Support Operational Partners. *Press Release (2016) 121.* North Atlantic Treaty Organization (NATO). Retrieved from http://nato.int/cps/en/natohq/official_texts_133171.htm?selectedLocale=en

Nelson, B. R. (2006). *The Making of the Modern State.* New York, Basingstoke: Palgrave Macmillan US.

OECD. (2007, April). *Principles for Good International Engagement in Fragile States & Situations.* Retrieved April 25, 2017, from OECD : http://www.oecd.org/dac/governance-peace/conflictfragilityandresilience/docs/38368714.pdf

OECD. (2008). *The OECD DAC Handbook on Security System Reform: Supporting Security and Justice.* Paris: OECD Publishing.

OECD. (2009, April 17). Concepts and dilemmas of State building in fragile situations: From fragility to resilience. *OECD Journal on Development, Vol. 9/3*, pp. 61–148.

OECD. (2010). *Do No Harm: International Support for Statebuilding.* Paris: OECD Publishing. doi:http://dx.doi.org/10.1787/9789264046245-en

OECD. (2011a). *International Engagement in Fragile States: Can't We Do Better?* Paris: OECD Publishing.

OECD. (2011b). Section 10: Monitoring and Evaluation. In *The OECD DAC Handbook on Security System Reform: Supporting Security and Justice.* Paris: OECD Publishing. doi:http://dx.doi.org/10.1787/9789264027862-13-en

Otłowski, T. (2014, December 31). *Afghanistan after the ISAF - how to avoid failure?* Retrieved April 24, 2017, from Pulaski Policy Papers. The Casimir Pulaski Foundation: https://pulaski.pl/wp-content/uploads/2015/02/Pulaski_Policy_Papers_No_17_14_EN.pdf

Porter, J. J. (2015). North Atlantic Treaty Organization: Transformation Under Fire. In G. A. Mattox, & S. M. Grenier (Eds.), *Coalition Challenges in Afghanistan: The Politics of Alliance* (pp. 184-198). Stanford: Stanford University Press.

Purcell, J., Martyris, D., Noor, N., & Rose, A. (2016, January). *Meta-Analysis of Final Evaluations of USAID Projects Implemented in Afghanistan, 2010-2015.* (U. A. Development, Ed.) Retrieved June 26, 2017, from USAID: http://pdf.usaid.gov/pdf_docs/PA00M8B2.pdf

Richmond, O. P. (2013). Failed Statebuilding versus Peace Formation. In T. D. David Chandler (Ed.), *Routledge Handbook of International Statebuilding* (pp. 130-140). Milton Park, Abingdon, Oxon: Routledge.

Rocha Menocal, A. (2011, November). State Building for Peace: A New Paradigm for International Engagement in Post-Conflict Fragile States? *Third World Quarterly*(32, no. 10), pp. 1715–1736. doi:10.1080/01436597.2011

Ruttig, T. (2015, November 08). *Dossier Afghanistan: Konfliktporträt.* Retrieved April 24, 2017, from Bundeszentrale für politische Bilding (bpb.de): http://www.bpb.de/internationales/asien/afghanistan/55517/konfliktportraet

Ruttig, T. (2016). Fluchtursachen und "sichere Schutzzonen" in Afghanistan. In M. Johannsen, B. Schoch, M. M. Mutschler, C. Hauswedell, & J. Hippler, *Friedensgutachten 2016* (pp. 114-126). Berlin: Lit Verlag Dr. W. Hopf.

Schetter, C. (2005, June). Warum zerfallen Staaten, und was genau passiert dabei? *Entwicklung und ländlicher Raum*, pp. 8-10.

Schetter, C. (2009). Die Taliban und die Neuordnung Afghanistans. In B. Chiari (Ed.), *Wegweiser zur Geschichte: Afghanistan* (pp. 83-99). Paderborn: Ferdinand Schöningh.

Schetter, C., & Mielke, K. (2016). Was von Kundus bleibt. Intervention, Gewalt und Soziale Ordnung in Afghanistan. *Politische Vierteljahreszeitschrift (PVS), 57*(4), pp. 614-642.

Schmidt, S. (2013). Good Governance als Entwicklungsvoraussetzung. In H. Ihne, & J. Wilhelm (Eds.), *Einführung in die Entwicklungspolitik* (pp. 284-290). Bonn: Bundeszentrale für politische Bildung (bpb).

Schnabel, A., & Born, H. (2011). *Security Sector Reform: Narrowing the Gap between Theory and Practice.* (A. Bryden, & H. Hänggi, Eds.) Geneva: The Geneva Centre for the Democratic Control of Armed Forces (DCAF).

Sedra, M. (2006, August 06). Security sector reform in Afghanistan: The slide towards expediency. *International Peacekeeping*, pp. 94-110.

Sedra, M. (2007). Security Sector Reform in Afghanistan: An Instrument of the State-Building Project. In L. Andersen, B. Møller, & F. Stepputat (Eds.), *Fragile States and Insecure People? Violence, Security, and Statehood in the*

Twenty-First Century (1 ed., pp. 151-176). New York (USA), Hampshire (UK): Palgrave Macmillan US.

Sedra, M. (2010). Diagnosing the Failings of Security Sector Reform in Afghanistan. *Sicherheit und Frieden (S+F) / Security and Peace, 4*(28), pp. 233-238.

Sisk, T. (2010). Paradoxes and Dilemmas of Democratization and State-Building in War-Torn Countries: From Problems to Policy. In J. Krause, & C. K. IV (Eds.), *International State Building and Reconstruction Efforts: Experience Gained and Lessons Learned* (pp. 57-75). Opladen & Farminton Hills, MI: Barbara Budrich Publishers.

Sisk, T. (2013). *Statebuilding: Consolidating Peace after Civil War.* Cambridge (UK); Malden (USA): Polity Press.

Sopko, J. F. (2016, February 12). *Assessing the Capabilities and Effectiveness of Afghan National Defense and Security Forces.* Retrieved August 25, 2017, from Special Inspector General for Afghanistan Reconstruction (SIGAR): https://www.sigar.mil/pdf/testimony/SIGAR-16-17-TY.pdf

Special Inspector General for Afghanistan Reconstruction (SIGAR). (2011, July 30). *Quarterly Report to the United States Congress.* Retrieved August 29, 2017, from SIGAR Special Inspector General for Afghanistan Reconstruction: https://www.sigar.mil/pdf/quarterlyreports/2011-07-30qr.pdf

Special Inspector General for Afghanistan Reconstruction (SIGAR). (2014a, February). *Afghan National Security Forces: Actions Needed to Improve Plans for Sustaining Capability Assessment Efforts.* Retrieved August 25, 2017, from SIGAR Special Inspector General for Afghanistan Reconstruction: https://www.sigar.mil/pdf/audits/SIGAR_14-33-AR.pdf

Special Inspector General for Afghanistan Reconstruction (SIGAR). (2014b, January). *Afghan National Security Forces: Despite Reported Successes, Concerns Remain about Literacy Program Results, Contract Oversight, Transition, and Sustainment.* Retrieved August 25, 2017, from SIGAR Special Inspector General for Afghanistan Reconstruction: https://www.sigar.mil/pdf/audits/SIGAR_14-30-AR.pdf

Special Inspector General for Afghanistan Reconstruction (SIGAR). (2017, July 2017). *Quarterly Report to the United States Congress.* Retrieved August 08, 2017, from SIGAR Special Inspector General for Afghanistan Reconstruction: https://www.sigar.mil/pdf/quarterlyreports/2017-07-30qr.pdf

Stevenson, A. (Ed.). (2010). *Oxford Dictionary of English* (3. Edition ed.). Oxford: Oxford University Press.

Stewart, P., & Emmott, R. (2017, June 29). *U.S. defense chief: U.S., allies withdrew from Afghanistan too fast.* Retrieved August 09, 2017, from Reuters:

http://www.reuters.com/article/us-nato-afghanistan-mattis-idUSKBN19K2PE

Stütz, J. (2008). *"State-Building" - aus theoretischer und praktischer Perspektive.* Baden-Baden: Nomos Verlag.

Tanner, S. (2012). *Afghanistan: A Military History from Alexander the Great to the War Against the Taliban* (Revised Edition ed.). Philadelphia: Da Capo Press.

The New York Times. (2017, August 21). *Full Transcript and Video: Trump's Speech on Afghanistan.* Retrieved September 22, 2017, from https://www.nytimes.com/2017/08/21/world/asia/trump-speech-afghanistan.html?mcubz=0

Tilly, C. (1985). War Making and State Making as Organized Crime. In P. B. Evans, D. R. Rhode Island, & T. Skocpol (Eds.), *Bringing the State Back In* (pp. 169-191). Cambridge: Cambridge University Press.

U.S. Army and U.S. Marince Corps. (2006, December 15). *Field Manual No. 3-24.* Washington, D.C.: Headquarter, Department of the Army. Retrieved from Headquarter Deparment of the Army: http://usacac.army.mil/cac2/Repository/Materials/COIN-FM3-24.pdf

U.S. Department of Defense (DOD). (2017, June). *Enhancing Security and Stability in Afghanistan.* Retrieved August 25, 2017, from RefID: 3-15EF0A8: https://www.defense.gov/Portals/1/Documents/pubs/June_2017_1225_Report_to_Congress.pdf

U.S. GAO. (2005, June). *Afghanistan Security: Efforts to Establish Army and Police Have Made Progress, but Future Plans Need to Be Better Defined.* Retrieved August 28, 2017, from GAO-05-575: http://www.gao.gov/new.items/d05575.pdf

U.S. GAO. (2009, April 21). *Afghanistan: Key Issues for Congressional Oversight.* Retrieved August 25, 2017, from GAO-09-473SP: https://www.gao.gov/assets/660/652075.pdf

U.S. GAO. (2011, January 27). *Afghanistan Security: Afghan Army Growing, but Additional Trainers Needed; Long-term Costs Not Determined.* Retrieved August 25, 2017, from GAO-11-66: https://www.gao.gov/assets/320/315200.pdf

U.S. GAO. (2012, July 24). *Afghanistan Security: Long-standing Challenges May Affect Progress and Sustainment of Afghan National Security Forces.* Retrieved August 25, 2017, from GAO-12-951T: https://www.gao.gov/assets/600/592913.pdf

U.S. GAO. (2013, February 11). *Afghanistan: Key Oversight Issues.* Retrieved August 25, 2017, from GAO-13-218SP: https://www.gao.gov/assets/660/652075.pdf

U.S. GAO. (2015, December 03). *Afghanistan: State and USAID Should Evaluate Actions Taken to Mitigate Effects of Attrition among Local Staff.* Retrieved August 25, 2017, from GAO-16-100: https://www.gao.gov/assets/680/673983.pdf

UNAMA. (2017, February). *Afghanistan. Protection of Civilians in Armed Conflict. Annual Report 2016.* Retrieved April 28, 2017, from United Nations Assistance Mission in Afghanistan (UNAMA): https://unama.unmissions.org/sites/default/files/protection_of_civilians_in_armed_conflict_annual_report_2016_final280317.pdf

United Nations. (2008, January 23). Securing peace and development: the role of the United Nations in supporting security sector reform. Report of the Secretary-General. *A/62/659–S/2008/39.* New York.

United Nations. (2013, August 13). Securing States and societies: strengthening the United Nations comprehensive support to security sector reform. Report of the Secretary-General. *A/67/970–S/2013/480.* New York.

United Nations Development Program (UNDP). (1994). *Human Development Report 1994.* Oxford, New York: Oxford University Press.

United Nations Educational, Scientific and Cultural Organization (UNESCO). (2016, September). *Case Study 4: The effects of police literacy training in Afghanistan.* Retrieved August 30, 2017, from Evaluation of UNESCO's Role in Emergencies and Protacted Crisis: http://unesdoc.unesco.org/images/0024/002464/246451E.pdf

Weber, M. (1946). Politics as a Vocation. In M. Weber, H. Gerth, & C. W. Mills, *From Max Weber: Essays in Sociology* (pp. 77-128). New York: Oxford University Press.

Webermann, J. (2017, April 22). *Afghanistan: Mehr als 140 Tote bei Taliban-Angriff.* Retrieved April 23, 2017, from tagesschau.de: https://www.tagesschau.de/ausland/afghanistan-taliban-angriff-fuenfzig-tote-103.html

Wieker, V. (2012). Afghanistan: Eine Bestandsaufnahme aus militärpolitischer Sicht – Ziele, Strategie und Perspektive des ISAF-Einsatzes. In A. Seiffert, P. C. Langer, & C. Pietsch (Eds.), *Der Einsatz der Bundeswehr in Afghanistan: sozial- und politikwissenschaftliche Perspektiven* (pp. 23-32). Wiesbaden: VS Verlag für Sozialwissenschaften.

Wilder, A. (2007, July). *Cops or Robbers?: The Struggle to Reform the Afghan National Police.* Retrieved April 04, 2017, from Afghanistan Research and Evaluation Unit (AREU): http://www.comw.org/warreport/fulltext/0707wilder.pdf

World Bank. (1997). *World Development Report 1997 : The State in a Changing World.* New York: Oxford University Press. Retrieved April 25, 2017, from https://openknowledge.worldbank.org/handle/10986/5980

World Bank. (2011). *World Development Report 2011: Conflict, Security, and Development.* Washington, DC: The World Bank. Retrieved April 25, 2017, from https://openknowledge.worldbank.org/handle/10986/5980

World Bank. (2012). *Guidance for Supporting State-Building in Fragile and Conflict-Affected States: A Tool-Kit.* Washington DC: The World Bank. Retrieved from The World Bank: http://siteresources.worldbank.org/PUBLICSECTORANDGOVERNANCE/Resources/285741-1343934891414/8787489-1347032641376/SBATGuidance.pdf

Zimmerman, S. R. (2015). The Afghan Government at War. In G. A. Mattox, & S. M. Grenier (Eds.), *Coalition Challenges in Afghanistan: The Politics of Alliance* (pp. 15-30). Stanford: Stanford University Press.

Zürcher, C. (2005, September). Gewollte Schwäche: Vom schwierigen analytischen Umgang mit prekärer Staatlichkeit. *Internationale Politik*, pp. 13-22.

Zeitfracht Medien GmbH
Ferdinand-Jühlke-Straße 7
99095 Erfurt, Deutschland
produktsicherheit@kolibri360.de